the HUSTLE ECONOMY

TRANSFORMING YOUR CREATIVITY INTO A CAREER

Edited by **Jason Oberholtzer**
Illustrated by **Jessica Hagy**

RUNNING PRESS
PHILADELPHIA · LONDON

© 2016 by Jason Oberholtzer and Jessica Hagy
Illustrations © 2016 by Jessica Hagy
Published by Running Press,
A Member of the Perseus Books Group

Books published by Running Press are available at special discounts for bulk purchases
in the United States by corporations, institutions, and other organizations. For more
information, please contact the Special Markets Department at the Perseus Books Group,
2300 Chestnut Street, Suite 200, Philadelphia, PA 19103, or call (800) 810-4145,
ext. 5000, or e-mail special.markets@perseusbooks.com.

ISBN 978-0-7624-6019-9
Library of Congress Control Number: 2015954073

E-book ISBN 978-0-7624-6027-4

9   8   7   6   5   4   3   2   1
Digit on the right indicates the number of this printing

Cover and interior design by Jason Kayser
Edited by Jason Oberholtzer and Jordana Tusman
Typography: Chronicle and Whitney

Running Press Book Publishers
2300 Chestnut Street
Philadelphia, PA 19103-4371

Visit us on the web!
www.runningpress.com

Contents

Introduction

JASON OBERHOLTZER, EDITOR AND PRODUCER
JESSICA HAGY, ARTIST AND WRITER

Welcome to now.

Creative careers don't start in the apocryphal mailroom. Real jobs are things our grandparents had, like pensions and segregated lunch counters. Tens of thousands of us are now working collections of gigs via networks knitted together with pixels and hope. Our job titles change daily, if not even more frequently. Our careers are DIY.

And we have more questions than answers. We are hustling to be viable. We are juggling and networking and contemplating and planning and learning as we go.

Because this is the new creative economy. This is the Hustle Economy. And we need all the help we can get.

That's why this book exists: Because even though we're all just winging it, we each know a little bit of something about making it (whatever *it* is) work. And maybe, together, we can all do a little bit more, a little bit better.

When we first started thinking about this anthology, we wanted to collect insights from people we respected and admired. We wanted voices that had been there, done that, and had the hand-stamps and

W-9s to prove it. We were looking for self-made hustlers who found their own voices and their own strides.

We wanted generous, honest, confessional voices. We wanted to get emotional essays, not dry business PowerPoints. We wanted all kinds of creative people with all kinds of backgrounds to pour their hearts out and tell their stories. We wanted diary entries, not case studies. We wanted to host a conference between covers.

And because anything done with heart and care is art, we wanted a wide spectrum of artists to present their ideas. We wanted to build a vibrant and noisy salon full of artists, writers, doers, hustlers, and worriers. Thinkers. Makers. Dancers. Founders. Wizards of self-made realms. People who put themselves out there and lived to tell about it.

Fortunately, when we approached these artists, they delivered. We got everything we wanted and more. We are humbled and stunned by the generosity and thoughtfulness of these essays, and by the caliber of the hustlers who jumped with us into this project.

The essays in this book are raw, honest, and real. Each touches on a different topic, a different take on what it means to be a creative in today's ever-changing and ever-infuriating economy. At the end of each essay, you will find suggested exercises to help make your creative work more rewarding and put your plans to action.

This collection is filled to the brim with solid advice, inspiration, and ideas, and is meant to give you both hope and pause. The essays are inspiring, funny, silly, and belligerent—just like the artists who wrote them. It is designed to help you think, create, and thrive.

We hope you get as much out of it as we have.

—Jason and Jessica

First Things First

NICK DOUGLAS,
COMEDY WRITER

Here's every Q&A about starting a career in the arts:

Aspiring creator: "How do I break in?"
Successful creator: "Just make good work and put it out there."

It's a smug cliché. It's frustrating and fatuous, and it's completely true.

What this seems to leave out is the making connections part and the "playing politics" part. But good news: You make the best connections by *just making good work and putting it out there.*

It is, in fact, who you know.

Connections are obviously important in creative fields. The best creative gigs aren't filled by job board applicants. Someone recommends one friend to another, or they've seen someone's work. The process isn't purely meritocratic, but it's actually very rarely nepotistic (no one wants to risk their reputation by recommending the wrong friend).

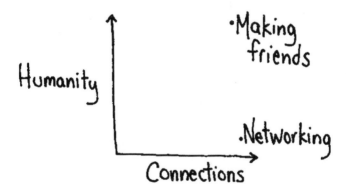

Building connections works the same way as building an audience: Over time, a creator convinces people that their work is consistently good, enough so that their next piece of work will be worth betting on. And even more than an audience, the right connections will feed into your talent.

Make good connections.

I think people imagine "making connections" as social climbing: You find the most famous people you can and try to make them pay attention to you so they can hand you their next opportunity. You're right to not want to do that. Don't.

Instead, make a different kind of connection: Find people you like, regardless of their status. This will make you feel less awkward, and it's much easier.

It's really rewarding when you can help people who are a little behind you in their career. Not selfishly, not to "earn points," but because you genuinely feel they deserve more opportunities than they have right now. So you hire them, or you refer them to a gig, or you make a project with them, or you promote their work. And you feel like you're doing everyone else a favor by showing them this underappreciated talent.

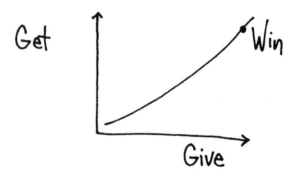

Almost all of the time, the people you help *will* get more opportunities. If they really have talent, you won't be the only one to notice and reward it. You'll see your colleagues succeed around and with you. Some will succeed faster. And if they actually like you, they'll want to help you out, too. Your assistant might hire you in five years.

How to collaborate.

Don't be afraid to ask people to collaborate *with* you. Most creative people *love* to be asked to join a project, and if they can't or don't want to, they'll probably be polite about declining.

If someone's an asshole, be overly polite back. Because occasionally you'll realize years later that *you* were the asshole: You were unclear, or the project was clearly not a fit for them, or you made the most common favor-asking mistake—you turned your request into a sales pitch.

I've seen hundreds of requests-as-pitches. They're transparent, and they make me feel like the requestor is hiding something. While you should clearly lay out the benefits to your would-be collaborator, don't be afraid to say how much their contribution would help *you*. And thank them during and after the project's completion. People want to help other people! They want to feel important to your project. And when they do, they're more likely to promote it.

Pick your collaborators by their talent, creative ambition, and ability to work with others. Their career status isn't important; that's the most fluid variable in any creative person's life. The absolute most valuable thing is to find people you want to work with over and over again. Whether or not you officially call yourselves a team, any time one of you gains a skill or connection, you will both benefit.

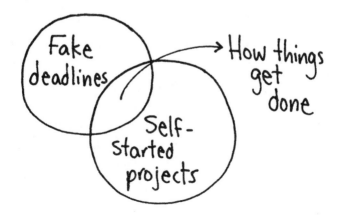

If you're the one who started a project, even if you've brought on an "equal partner," you'll probably be the one who pushes to finish it. But if you make a consistent schedule with your collaborator, you'll both find it harder to slack off. That's especially helpful for projects with no real deadline—just keep making new deadlines and be driven by the terror of disappointing your partner. This is normal. Fake deadlines are secretly why anyone finishes anything.

Market your stuff, stupid.

"Putting it out there" primarily means marketing your work. And it's more important than simply giving an update on your latest piece. Most of the best creative gigs come from a client or an audience who already knows who you are. So when you publicize your existing work, you're also publicizing your future work.

You're building an identity (which people can follow, because you, of course, have active profiles on your audience's preferred social networks). You're taking the "what you know" that you put into your work, and turning it into "who you know."

"Putting it out there" also means marketing unfinished work, which is often the real legwork that subsidizes the fun bits: auditioning, pitching, applying, submitting, fund-raising. It's asking people to pay, through purchase, pledge, commission, or paycheck, for what you'll make next.

As Kickstarter has demonstrated, asking people for money can be a great way to introduce them to your work. But pre-marketing works best when the recipient has already heard of you—which is why it gets easier the longer you've been around.

Extroverts get an "unfair" advantage because they make themselves approachable. They actually talk to their fans; they might even get the fans to interact with each other independently (the real difference between an audience and a community). They can present themselves as normal people. That makes it easier for others to imagine reaching out to them. And you really need to strike people as someone worth reaching out to.

"Just"

"*Just* make good work and put it out there." That first word doesn't mean "simply," it means "only." Don't procrastinate, don't hide your work. And don't make bad work, at least not knowingly.

In his YouTube video "Protect Your Love of Your Work," poet Steve Roggenbuck warns that if you compromise your work to expand your audience, "to one degree or another you will successfully reach other people. But once those people are surrounding you, they're going to want more and more of what drew them, which was a compromised version of you." And you will have less passion to make it for them.

That doesn't mean don't listen to criticism or never accept limitations or never do a gig for money. It just means don't give up something you value in your own work just to attract people who currently aren't interested in you. That's what it means to be a hack. And as with audiences, so with collaborators and connections.

Don't make the connections you think you have to make; they'll lead you toward work you didn't want to do, and that's already the easiest work to get. Make connections by doing your favorite thing with others' help, and eventually you'll get asked to do it again with a bigger budget, or paycheck, or audience.

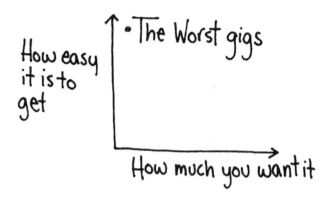

Working for free.

Creative work is undervalued. Clients underpay, customers pirate, tax systems are poorly structured—capitalism all around is mostly shitty to all but the most successful creative artists. And you shouldn't work for free as often as people want you to.

But you will have to do *some* work for free. The thing about skilled work is that you have to develop the skill before it's worth money. (And just because you've gotten paid before doesn't mean you'll always get paid again.) But this is the work you do to get known.

You show some forward momentum: You show that the next thing will be better. You take every gig you can, because the worst gig can still introduce you to the person who will hire you for the best gig.

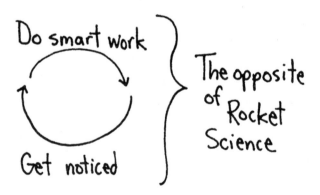

"Overnight success" means nothing but "I missed their early work." And your early work is where you meet the people you'll work with for the rest of your life.

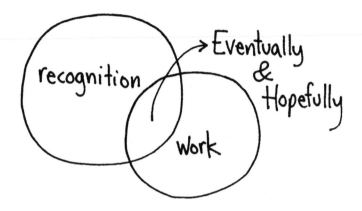

Act on This

Spend at least fifteen minutes making something new today. Make your work public on the same day you create it.

* * *

Tomorrow, spend at least twenty minutes making something better than what you made today.

* * *

Repeat until you are magnificently talented.

Direction, Success, and You

JASON OBERHOLTZER,
EDITOR AND PRODUCER

There are two types of hustling. The first type is when you know what you want to do with your life and pursue that dream however possible, inside or outside the system. Whether your dreams reside in the board-room or by the easel, you know what you want and you chase it.

The second type of hustling involves not knowing the specifics of what you want to do, rather having a sense that you'd like to be inter-ested in your work and be in charge of yourself. Any one path does not hold the answer, and no specific dream compels your longing.

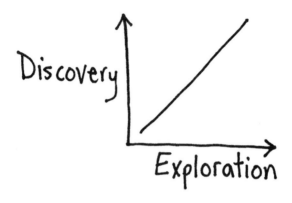

I am the second type of hustler. I don't have a career in the tradi-tional sense. What I do have is a résumé full of varied projects and an ever-changing set of skills that has been cobbled together as those skills have been required of me over the years. And I've found that, in this economy, varied projects, interests, and skills constitute a career.

Thanks to the wealth of available knowledge and training the Inter-net provides, the decreasing cost of equipment (a lot of which is now software, where it once was bulky, expensive hardware), and the ease of working remotely, the barrier to entry for most kinds of work (at least the fun work where you don't need advanced degrees . . . yawn) has never been lower. This of course assumes you have time and energy remaining to work on whatever you want to work on, after you have spent time and energy supporting yourself financially—which is obviously the trickiest part of the equation, so forgive me a lengthy digression....

This book is filled with essays written by talented, driven, ~successful~ people. "Successful" gets zazz tildes and scare quotes because honestly, what does "successful" even mean?

To avoid further digression, let's just stick with a simple definition: ~*~Success~*~ is a state that requires entry through achievement, the terms of which are entirely subjective. The people in this book are empirically talented and driven, and are rendered #successful by some very special magic. I suspect the way most people see it, a component integral in that magic is financial stability. Lo, the blessed market has proven that, yes, these people do indeed belong here.

So, how did they get here? And what exactly does "here" look like? Living month-to-month off gigs? Having some savings? A path to retirement? Accumulated wealth? When are you making enough money doing something to say you've arrived?

On the one hand, this is a great and pragmatic series of questions worth looking at. On the other hand, I don't think it's a topic often spoken about very honestly. And I suspect most of us are inaccurate with our assessments of the financial lives of those around us, especially those we look up to. My experience suggests that the stability and self–support–ability of the successful set is frequently and wildly exaggerated.

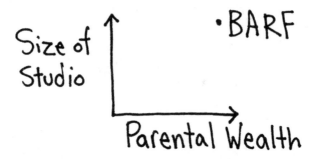

The contours of "here" are different for each person in this book. By and large, we are all still working at our craft and at our ability to support ourselves. Most of us have seen some lean months. Why does this matter? Beyond it being true, it's related to the issue of having time and energy to work on whatever you want to work on, once you've taken care of your finances. The finances of the creative set are generally not as stable or as verdant as you'd imagine them to be, which means that you might not be as far removed from that set as you might think.

It would be misleading to say this means the only thing standing between you and having your essay in this collection is being comfortable with unstable finances. There's more involved. However, neither privilege nor struggle fully captures the journey to "here." The typical journey is part willingness to get by with less at times, part luck, and part grace—in different proportions for different people.

Could you get by with half your current income? Could you get to a place where you make that much in your dream profession before your runway of savings runs out? These are the types of questions involved in making "the leap" into the hustle and staying in the hustle, far more frequently than questions about passion and ability. Most people have passion, and ability can be enhanced. What gets tested most often is the ability to sit with discomfort and uncertainty. The skill most used is that of finding different ways to see progress and success.

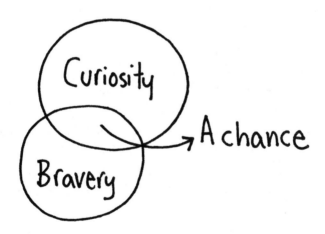

What I'm trying to get at is that nobody really makes it to ~*~success~*~. Everyone rises and falls in patterns throughout their life. Being involved in the hustle isn't about arriving anywhere—it's about being in the mix. Further, the hustle isn't even about people who are great at being in the mix, who have captured bits of wisdom and live them, who are financially stable and generally adored. There aren't many people like that. So, if you're in the mix, you are already there, you are successful.

What does this all mean about marshaling the time and energy to work on what you actually want to work on? It certainly doesn't intend to ignore that there are people who do not have access to sufficient time or energy. That is a practical reality and a tremendous challenge to the spirit—nobody in these positions should be made to feel shame. They are not ignoring their calling or too scared to take a chance on themselves; they are simply living their lives responsibly and admirably.

The intention of all this money talk is to suggest that maybe the successful set aren't all that far removed from the rest of us. Maybe they don't actually make that much more money than us, or produce that much more output than those among us who consider ourselves something, well, less successful.

OK, digression concluded—let's get back to the second type of hustle: the career of varied projects.

When you aren't focused in one area, building specific, marketable experience and skill, you are cultivating another broader skill: getting good at getting good at things. Climbing a lot of steep learning curves doesn't so much make you good at all the peaks you reach; rather, it makes you good at climbing those curves quickly and efficiently. That is your skill as the broadly interested hustler.

Back to me for a moment, for context. In the last year, as of this writing, I've worked on this book, released a free jazz album based on a science fiction novel, helped produce a friend's singer-songwriter album, edited a video series of watch commercials, hosted and edited a podcast, written a screenplay, developed content strategy for a Fortune 25 company, written a market research report, researched soccer fandom habits for an Italian soccer club, headed a product team developing a prototype for a professional networking startup, and curated a blog about charts.

Regrets you carry

Opportunities you embrace

Most of these things I was doing for the first time. There are overlapping skill-sets and technical knowledge and wisdom I can take with me from one place to another, but each process was relatively new to me when I set out. And that's why I do this! That's what brings me joy. If you are this second type of hustler, this is hopefully what will bring you joy, too.

The projects I've worked on this past year each served a different purpose. Some work makes you money, some reaches an audience (of peers, fans, whatever), and some you feel is actually good work, for its own sake. Your favorite projects will hit two of these checkboxes; the ones you will remember forever hit all three. It's totally fine doing things that hit only one.

Rather than beat myself up about what any particular project *isn't*, I try to ask myself three questions: (1) Did it make me money? (2) Did it reach people? (3) Did it feel like something I took pride in? This is the sort of math you do when your career involves doing a little bit of everything you can.

So now, let's get down to some concrete advice.

First, get shit done.

What you make won't always be good, make you money, or reach your desired audience. But if you finish it, it will at the very least be done. And that matters. That's the only way it has a chance of checking any of those boxes. Do things. Do them until they are done. Then do other things.

Say yes to everything until you have specific experience to call on as to why you should be saying *no*. When a good idea comes along, jump on it. And while you're waiting, make other things—don't wait around.

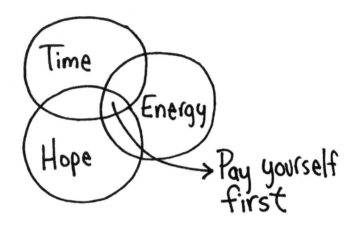

As much as possible, embrace that which motivates you to action rather than that which taxes your energy so much that its toxic energy reaches into other areas. This includes your projects as well as your business relationships.

Relationships and communities are stronger than individuals, so collaborate. Invite people into what you are making. Find people whom you think more clearly or creatively around, and work with them. Find people who are good at getting things done, and promise each other you will do things. Social pressure works wonders!

Invest in yourself in concrete ways.

Learn new tangible skills. Invest in the resources around you—new hardware, new software—not extravagantly or without a direction, but with a plan for what you will make and how it will reward you. To remind you again, the reward doesn't always have to be monetary. Experience, visibility, résumé material, new relationships, and simple joy are all valid payback for investing in yourself.

Find patterns.

For whatever reason, opportunities tend to arrive in clumps and dry seasons are always dry.

Have a relationship with your anxiety.

Like pain, a little bit of anxiety is uncomfortable but is usually there to help. It can often point you to what you are overlooking or what needs to be done first. That said, it's also sometimes totally wrong and unintelligible, in which case tell it to shut up, and keep moving!

Often your confusion, frustration, ennui, or lack of motivation or creativity is the gig's fault more than your own. It can be very difficult to identify when this is the case. At least be open to the possibility.

Set up your email, to-do list, and calendar.

It's worth the calories you'll save later to get this stuff locked down. Try a new system every few months until something sticks—then reinvent as needed.

Finally, you're going to fuck up all these rules. Please forgive yourself.

Act on This

Find a new type of hustle. Make a list of projects
or areas of interest related to what you do
(but not exactly what you do) and that you
haven't tried yet.

✳ ✳ ✳

Figure out a natural first starting point.
Want to write a book? Write a chapter. Want to start a
business? Make a business plan.

✳ ✳ ✳

Make sure you are able to finish the projects,
even (especially) if they are just for your own edification.
Then, see how taking a bigger bite the next
time feels to you. You might just open up a
new area of work for yourself.

The Wily Octopus

BEN GRELLE (AKA THE FROGMAN),
INTERNET COMEDIAN, WRITER,
PHOTOGRAPHER, AND GRAPHIC ARTIST

The plan was to be famous all along. My chubby, fourteen-year-old self had certainties of grandeur. I dare not call them delusions, because I knew I had a juggernaut-like potential that could not be stopped. I was good at making people laugh. I studied comedy like it was a science, and at the age of eighteen, I headed off to college to study theater and secretly begin my career as a stand-up comic.

But everything changed when the Fire Nation attacked.

We are taught from a young age that we have a say in our destiny, that our dreams are all attainable. A part of me still really believes that. But what I didn't realize is that as time passes, our dreams are often transformed into something we wouldn't have recognized earlier, like a wily octopus that takes the shape of whatever space it ends up in.

I had three months of college under my belt, and I had gone to three classes. I could barely feed myself, and when I did, I derived all my nutrition from microwave nuggets. Ambiguous chicken parts were sustaining me. I was so . . . tired.

This was not your average tired. This was not missing a few hours of sleep. This was not the fatigue after a long night of imbibing spirits. This felt exceedingly wrong. Something in my body had broken, and it kept getting worse.

I dropped out of college and moved back in with my parents. I tried to work at a job, but I couldn't handle even part-time. I'd sneak out on nights when my body was more cooperative and do a set at whatever club/bar/establishment would let me tell my super-extra-funny jokes.

I could feel the dream that I had as a teenager slipping away. My failing body was no longer under my control, and the energy required to do an effective performance soon became impossible to attain. Not only was my body broken, but this crushing disappointment broke my mind as well.

The doctors told me what I had could not be fixed. The psychiatrists tried to repair my mind, but for a long time I retreated to a dark bedroom and stopped existing. My purpose was to make people laugh. My dream was to do it on a grand scale. I felt like a useless husk. A great potential wasted.

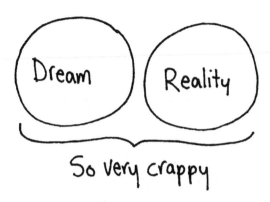

What I didn't realize at the time was that my dream was still possible. I was just being a very stubborn octopus. I only wanted my dream to take the form I had first imagined, instead of allowing it to take the shape of the space provided. I could still perform my function. I could still serve my purpose. I just had to do it in a way that was copacetic with my circumstances.

Enter the Internet. Stage right.

I was part of a tiny, geeky social network. We would lament about poorly conceived computer operating systems. We would brag about our "gaming rigs." We would say things like "overclocking" and "I don't think anyone is going to buy that iPhone thing." I started making friends on this site, and as we conversed, my comments were met with LOLs. This feeling was familiar. It wasn't a room full of drunken strangers guffawing at my poop joke, but this was still laughter. The digital audience reaction was just as intoxicating as I remembered. I wanted more. People were all, "LMAO," and I was like, "Reattach your buttocks so I can make them fall off again with my jokes!"

I began crafting more complicated bits of humor. I would head to Photoshop to create visual gags to further impress my techno-cronies.

In comes a fellow named Truett McGowan. We began chatting in a little box in the corner of Gmail. He encouraged me, helped me work out ideas, and even participated in the tomfoolery. When I was feeling down, he propped me up on his shoulders. I kept telling him about my dreams of performing in front of people and how I didn't think they were possible.

He verbally bitch slapped me and told me I was already performing in front of people that very second. I was making people laugh just as I had on that stage, fulfilling my purpose just as I was meant to. It may not have been the same platform that I envisioned, but I was reaching people and making them smile. Many of those people really needed that.

Truett soon forced me to make something called a "Tumblr." I was apprehensive; I don't like things that are missing vowels. If I learned anything from watching *Wheel of Fortune* with my grandma, it was that vowels have value.

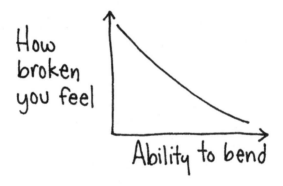

I began doing my antics for the people of Tumblr. It was slow going at first. I cherished every note. Every re-blog. I was no longer making just my friends laugh—I was trying to reach strangers.

Day by day, follower by follower, my audience began to grow—at a snail's pace, at first. And I failed a lot. Terrible things I made would enter the abyss of the Internet. Maybe one in ten would hit its mark. But I learned from those failures and kept going.

I eventually got that number to three in ten.

Then five in ten.

Then seven in ten.

It took me two years to learn how to make consistently funny material. But one day, being funny was no longer enough. This was an entirely different medium from stand-up, and I had to relearn how to be funny using the tools of the Internet. Once I finally felt like I had it figured out, the next step was to get more ambitious with my material. One fateful day, I made an animated gif. At the time, this was a relatively new thing on Tumblr. I was probably one of the first to use it as a tool for original content.

In one of my first gifs, Will Smith and Tommy Lee Jones are in their *Men in Black* costumes. They put on their sunglasses.

Then I try to put on my sunglasses in the same suave motion.

Quickly, one hundred comments rolled in. Then a thousand. Then ten thousand. The gif ended up on every popular site you could imagine. Soon enough it was literally seen by millions of people.

Story over, right? I achieved success and lived happily ever after. Smooth sailing from then on.

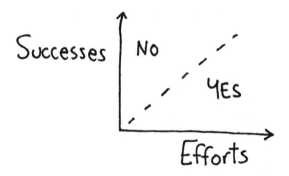

The truth is this: That's when the hard work actually started. That bit of fame was an opportunity. It gave me an opening to build an audience and gain their loyalty. I had to make more gifs, Photoshops, articles—anything I could think of. You can't take one popular thing you make and ride it to success. You have to double your efforts and keep making cool things. As for me, I had to do my best to reach that bar I set for myself again and again.

And I was happy to try. My efforts made droves of people smile. I was fulfilling my purpose, doing what I was meant to do. I was entertaining more people than I could have ever done with stand-up. And while I certainly miss the live energy of having the laughter in the same room, I realize that I am reaching more people and impacting their lives in a profound way. It's not a huge compromise to live without performing live.

So here is the part where I start summing up what you should have learned from my tale of woe and success: You have to be patient and persistent. Think about how long it should take to achieve success and prepare for that time to be quadrupled. Or octupled. Or whatever comes after octupled.

You will suck at first. You will suck a lot. Experience is the only way to stop sucking. Do not see your failures as failures. They are learning opportunities. They will teach you so much more than your successes. Keep failing until you don't anymore.

A single success is just an open door. It is not a free ride to happy town. Anything worth doing is tons of work. From when you wake up to when you go to sleep, and weekends, too. When that door opens, that is when you start working your patoot off. And when your patoot falls off, staple it back on until you work it off again.(This essay has a lot of stuff about butts falling off, but I am OK with that.)

The most important lesson is to be like the wily octopus. Having a dream is an amazing thing. Many people don't know what their dream is. If you have one, consider yourself one of the lucky ones. But when you try to achieve that dream, please, *please* don't be rigid and stubborn. Don't form it in a way that can only take one shape. It needs to be an octopus. It needs to take the shape of whatever your circumstances may be.

All I truly wanted was to make people laugh, and I thought that that absolutely needed to happen on a stage in front of a microphone. I resisted changing the shape of my dream for so long, and it only led to depression and misery. The moment my friend Truett showed me there was another way to achieve my dream—if only I let it change shape—my life changed forever.

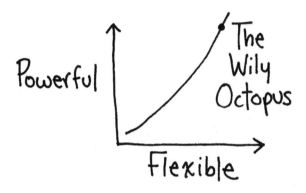

Not all of you will have a Truett McGowan. So allow me to be that kick-in-the-ass you need, right now. Break down what you want to achieve into its simplest form and start from there. Wander around as your shape-changing octopus self. Experiment and work hard. Send your dreams to all the places you can think of. And eventually, I think you'll find a place where you fit just right. Your wily octopus will mold into that shape and become a reality.

Act on This

You're reading this book for a reason.

* * *

You need something.

* * *

Maybe you need a critical nudge, a map to get to your next role, or some words of encouragement.

* * *

And while a book can guide you, it can't answer *all* of your questions.

* * *

So get what you need: Ask the Internet for help.

* * *

Email your family. Post an honest and not even a little bit humble-braggy message on Facebook.

* * *

Drop a message into a bottle in the form of a tweet. Message the universe however you prefer.

* * *

Someone out there will probably reply with your answers.

* * *

And if they don't? Keep asking until they do. The Internet never shuts off.

In Defense of the Hustle

ADRIAN SANDERS,
COFOUNDER OF BEACON

Recently there's been a lot of discussion and mounting criticism about the "hustle" life. Most of the talking points focus on working long hours, taking on too much stress at once, and the (really, truly) stupid belief that going "110 percent" will guarantee riches. Real tragedies both public and private abound in no small part due to these beliefs, especially now as seed startups are biting the dust from the boom of 2011.

But why all this criticism focused on the hustle?

There are plenty of real problems in startup land: the herd mentality, the general dilution of talent and unique perspectives, the misogyny bro-culture, the disconnect from the 99 percent, and so on. But hustling is not one of these problems. If anything, there's not enough of it in startups. For me, the hustle has never been about working long hours or working harder than anyone else. I think in no small part, there is a misinterpretation of exactly what the hustle is.

Here are some commonly accepted definitions of "hustle":

To make money by any means necessary, legal or otherwise.

To feign a lack of skill while bets are made before a game of skill starts.

To move energetically or dynamically in a competitive activity.

Hustling in hip hop is a deeply American cultural construct. Money is everything. Do anything to get money. Hustling in skill competitions is a celebration of cunning, guile, and hacking the rules of the game. Hustling in sports is the 110-percent effort of giving it your all for the whole match.

In each of these cases, the hustle represents the act of doing whatever is necessary to achieve a singular goal: Win. Hustling epitomizes a very focused (even myopic) obsession with winning. No matter what happens, the hustler will try anything and everything to succeed.

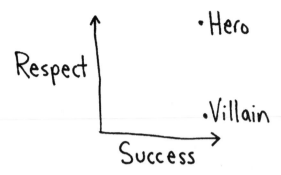

Hustling is never explicitly the sole act of working insanely hard, working insanely smart, lying, cheating, stealing, coercing, finagling, or scamming—even if we associate these things with the term. In the hustler's mind, the "hustle" occurs when you win. The means are merely different methods to the madness.

Some hustlers do work hard, and some work smart. They can be morally ambiguous at best, greedy at worst, but above all, self-serving. In startup land, venture capitalists love them because they represent the type of ego-driven, power- and cash-hungry personas that map well to histories of exits and profit. It's not a guarantee of success, but it's certainly a good sign.

As you may have read in hundreds of articles online, the life of a hustler is a bunch of bullshit. The chances of it paying out are slim, and given the appetite for risk required, they're not even possible for most Americans. Instead you burn out, your personal life craters, and your perspective on what it means to be a living, breathing human being fades. Above all, you focus entirely on winning—a ridiculously arbitrary notion of merit, and yet a very persistent one.

So why defend the hustle?

Hustling is a big fuck-you to everything that stands in the hustler's way. Hustlers actively perpetuate the Horatio Alger myth of rags to riches, a blatant lie about what is possible in America (statistically speaking).

Occasionally, outside the bounds of the system, some of them succeed, and things are forever changed for better and worse.

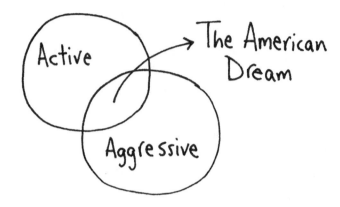

The hustle is when you spend all your PayPal exit money on absurd dreams of the stars and electric cars. It's when you burn the park benches to keep the fire alive in your studio. It's when you cook down leather boots for food in the winter. Hustling is defending yourself with the frying pan. It's Odysseus outsmarting the Cyclops. It's stealing the wrestling captain's girl while you're giving her math lessons. Nothing celebrates the potential impact of a single human being quite like the hustle.

The hustle is also when you sacrifice everything, and nothing works out. It's Escobar in jail, Enron, the financial industry over the past twenty years, Color for iPhone. It's a yellow brick road littered with suicides, alcoholism, abuse, fraud, and reckless abandon.

We love hustlers, especially in America. We recite Steve Jobs' famous quote, "Good artists copy, great artists steal," re-watch the Larry Bird diving-out-of-bounds-behind-his-head assist, and listen to the Jay Z mythologies of getting out of the ghetto.

It should be noted that none of these people come off as kindhearted, empathetic individuals. They only care about winning. We appreciate their singular, driven goals clearly. We know that they wear not hearts, but dreams, on their sleeves. We admire their gumption. Their necessity is clear. And their invention is always genuine. Inside every hustle is the soul of a determined individual filled with irrational belief.

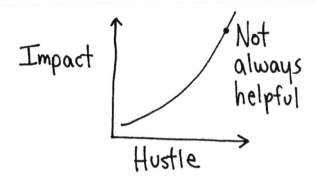

Hustlers are rule benders and breakers. They push the boundaries of what we think is acceptable and possible. They are often the ones pushing the human condition forward *and* backward. When they're good, they're great. When they're bad, they're asshole lobbyists tanking our country.

Above all, to hustle is to cause change.

It is bending and breaking rules to achieve something in spite of the odds. You could argue that hustlers are the only real agents of change. Tesla may have invented a bunch of cool stuff, but Edison was the jerk who brought it to millions of people.

When we admire hustlers, something clicks inside each of us. We are compelled to appreciate ingenuity and persistence in the pursuit of singular goals. Forces greater than our individual will are constantly at work against us, and so we cheer on the Stampers to make their log run. We believe in miracles on ice, buzzer beaters, and muses for playwrights and startups because we want all those people to win. In

America, everyone loves the kid with the lemonade stand in the summer and the sweet, smiling troublemakers in high school who sell lunch tickets for booze money (sorry, Mom).

But, if the hustle is basically some antiquated primal element of our psyche, shouldn't we, in our comfortable, sophisticated society, work to abolish it?

Consider the creation of an individual human and all the processes and events required for this new person to exist. On the top level there is a tremendous amount of hustle from two individuals. But even before this, you must factor in six billion people, multiply by time and geography, then add a bunch of circumstance, and there's still so much work to do!

There's that one egg that's got to make that trip (unscathed no less!), and then there's that one sperm that will need to triumph over so many peers (among other obstacles). After all of this, there's still the mother's own will to persevere, and then the child's first moments in the world—kicking, struggling, and finally crying out to announce her presence. And then she will need to get through middle school.

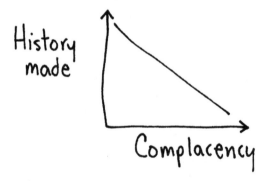

Human conception, conscious life as we know it, is just a culmination of a bunch of random separate entities that got what they wanted. So while you certainly can kick back and enjoy the life, please recognize that you can't knock the hustle.

Act on This

Now is the time to articulate what you want.

* * *

What.

YOU.

Want.

* * *

Success is a generic word, but your version of it is probably very specific. Define your definition of "making it." Add bullet points. Throw in some concrete aspects like dates and dollar amounts.

* * *

Now that you know exactly where you want to go, you can actually make plans to get there.

On Having It All Figured Out

FARAH KHALID,
FILM EDITOR

OK, I've been here before. There's nothing to worry about, no need to panic. I'm not going to die, right? I'm not going to starve. The last job I had will NOT be the last job I will EVER have. . . .

But I'm such a failure. All these other people are so good—why can't I be like them? They even look happier. They have it all figured out. What the hell is wrong with me? Who will hire me again? I'm just not good enough.

I'm not good enough. I'm not good enough. I'm not good enough.

And on and on and on. The phrase repeats in my head like a meditation mantra, hammering down my ego before the world has a chance to. Who do I think I am, that I can be something special?

I'm not good enough. The voice reminds me that I'm fooling myself, and only myself, because the world already knows I'm not good enough. I'm not one of *them*. You know, *them*—the *cool* people, the *successful* people, the ones who have it all figured out.

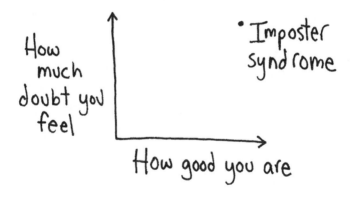

This is how I spent most of my youth and all of my twenties: fleeting moments of confidence wrapped in long, drawn-out epidemics of panic and dread.

It started with the cool people at school. I was definitely *not* one of them, and they made sure to remind me of it every single day: *You're not pretty enough; you're not cool enough; you're not good enough.* From there, it was just ingrained in me: Some people are cool and have it all figured out, and others don't and won't ever. I was the latter.

I spent most of my life thinking there was a collective *they,* a group that was a close-knit society that seemed to gather wherever I wanted to be, physically and metaphorically. I knew in reality there wasn't any sort of group, but I couldn't shake the feeling that somehow the in-crowd was everywhere. My fictitious Illuminati congregated in clubs I was trying to get into, new industries I was trying to get in on the ground floor of, even in my circles of friends. I could not escape *them* nor did I want to. I wanted to be one of them. I wanted to have it all figured out.

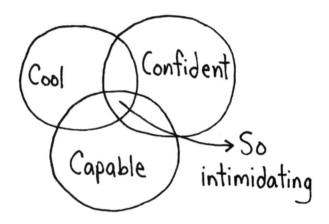

What really bothers me now is that in 18+ years of school, no one ever told me that no one has it figured out—not the cheerleader who gets all the guys, not the guy who gets all the cheerleaders, not the straight-A student, the valedictorian, the teacher, the principal, the world-famous rock star, the doctor, the artist, the agent, the movie star, the author, the entrepreneur—nobody.

As a film editor, I've worked intimately with all types of people, from living legends to young up-and-coming artists. I now know this to be a constant truth: We are all insecure beings, no matter how successful we are. And I believe the more successful you become, the more criticism you receive (more people are around to criticize you), and the greater your insecurity becomes. No one is shielded from it. Some of the most successful people I've ever met are also some of the most insecure.

As humans, we are raised to doubt ourselves. It starts the very first time someone tells us we shouldn't do something we thought was perfectly fine. It ingrains in us that the rules and opinions of society are the final judges of our actions, so we must always look to society for approval. These early interactions teach us that our instincts may not be trustworthy. In reality, our instincts are what make us unique, special, and desirable as a human being and as an artist. We should always trust our instincts, especially creatively.

Had I learned this concept earlier in my life, I could have avoided a multitude of panic attacks and a fortune in therapy bills. My post-college adulthood has been a process of expunging everything I learned growing up and erasing all the negativity and criticism I received as a child.

I grew up a skinny brown girl in a small, primarily white town in New Jersey, in the 1980s, when there were barely any brown people on TV or in the news. I was teased for my skin color, my features, and my clothes (which admittedly did *sometimes* smell like curry). I never had any boy interested in me. I wasn't invited to any of the cool birthday parties. I was a pariah and I accepted it. I accepted it for way too long.

Of course, I'm no aberration—everyone has their childhood demons—but we need to recognize that they are just that. And those demons need to be led out into the light and obliterated.

My life started on a very normal path. I had no idea what I wanted to become, so I applied to UC Berkeley in the hopes of getting a safety-net business degree just like my elder sister had. By luck, Berkeley sort of rejected me and sent me to a community college for my first two years, with guaranteed deferred admission, barring any academic mishaps.

In community college I stumbled upon a cinema club, where all the students seemed to be lost souls like myself, who had found a passion for film and were doing it. People my age were making actual films. Mind you, this was before the age of cell phones, digital technology, electricity, and cars—well, almost.

In my head, filmmakers were always an exclusive group of highly trained, innately talented individuals who jumped straight from the womb into the director's chair. They were part of the Illuminati. When I realized this wasn't the case and that this field was accessible to me, I knew I wanted it.

It was love at first sight, and I loved everything about it: the creativity, the group dynamics, the terminology (like how a clothespin is not a clothespin, but a C-47); it was all very exciting and self-important. Who doesn't like saying, "I'm sorry, I can't. I have to be on set tomorrow"? I felt like an insider at last.

From then on, it was just a bunch of trial and error resulting in plenty of failure. I became vice president of the cinema club. I bought a super 8 film camera and a splicing machine. I relinquished my pseudo admission to UC Berkeley and applied to UCLA and USC film schools. Both schools rejected me for the film program, but USC accepted me as an undecided, also known as "film-school-in-waiting" because that's what all the undecided majors were.

At USC, I took every class on film I could and applied again to the film program. I was accepted as a Critical Studies student in the film school—which was basically foot-in-the-door-but-still-waiting-for-the-production-program. After all, I wanted to make movies, not sit around and criticize them. So I took a film class that the dean of admissions happened to be teaching.

Luckily for me it was a small class of about twenty students. Even luckier for me, the dean of admissions offered office hours for her students, so I scheduled a meeting and told her of my lofty goals to become a production student and a filmmaker. Now she knew my name, my face, and my goals. Next semester when I applied for the third time, I was finally accepted as a Production major, the acceptance letter signed by the very same dean of admissions. Cue the applause.

In all this time, however, I never recognized that I was hustling. I just had a goal and I did what I could to achieve it. I also never knew I was networking; I was just talking to people and telling them what I hoped to do. At school they had always ingrained in us the importance of networking, which scared me to death. What is networking? How am I supposed to do it? What am I supposed to say? I had nervous fits at the thought of Networking with a capital "N." It took me years to realize that Networking is just talking. It is no more than that. That's the big secret. I'm still not the best at it and I hate it abstractly, but most networking events have free wine and food, so that always helps ease the awkwardness.

I obtained my first job out of college much in the same way. I wasn't ever really hired so much as I forced my way in (sweetly of course). I was an intern for an editor/director, and she badly needed an assistant but didn't know it. After a few months of interning and right before graduation, I told her that she would lose me as an intern since I needed to get a job, unless she wanted to hire me because she really needed an assistant. So I was hired. I was brought in as an assistant editor and as her personal assistant on a per-project basis. Thus began my freelance life.

When I first started life out of school, a friend gave me a journal as a present. Inside, he had written out Robert Frost's famous poem "The Road Not Taken." That poem became the adage by which I lived. In my moments of hesitation and doubt, I would open that journal and reread that poem to remind myself to keep on going.

It's been fifteen years now and I'm still going strong, but even as I write this, a little voice in my head whispers, "I hope so." Thanks, voice, thanks for reminding me you are always there to doubt me.

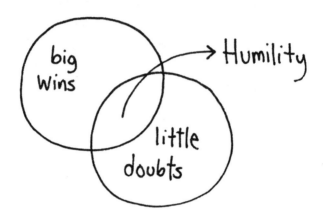

The voice also brings up a good point: Things never become certain in this lifestyle, but the flip side is that they also never become mundane. You never know where you are going to be or what you are going to be working on. I've worked in LA, NY, Atlanta, Puerto Rico, Paris, and Morocco, on a train to D.C., in a Border's bookstore café, in many a hotel room in random towns, in a mansion in Greenwich, CT, on a private jet somewhere over the Atlantic Ocean, in a car on the way to the airport for a flight I was not going on, and at home—lots and lots of jobs from home. So that's the reward for all the uncertainty—excitement, adventure, and always something new.

The only constant you will have is that little voice. Even though it never goes away, over the years, you manage to lower its volume and wave it off with a dismissive laugh. To this day, every time I start a new job or work with a new client, that voice returns, attempting to remind me: *I will fail! I am not good enough. I can't do this job; this is out of my league.* It's not always easy to let it go or laugh it off, but it's gotten easier.

I've learned to acknowledge this voice as a manifestation of my fear. After fear comes growth, so it's good. It means I'm challenging myself with this new project. It means I have to do it because being afraid is never a reason not to try something. If you don't have fear, it means you are not pushing yourself out of your comfort zone, you are not changing, and you are just playing it safe.

Fear can be an indicator of when you need to push yourself harder. When were you last afraid/uncomfortable? Not recently? Well then, are you really growing as an artist? No real goals are ever accomplished without fear—it's a main ingredient. Fear is part of this lifestyle, so embrace it. Take it to dinner and get comfy with it, because if you want this life, fear is always going to be there. But just remember that it can also be your best friend.

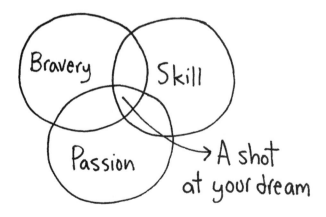

So that's it, that's the big mystery behind the curtain. If you are good at what you do, passionate about it, and brave enough to stick it out, you will succeed. There will be many, many moments when you might want to give up and take the easier route, but don't. Take the road not taken.

Act on This

Find your people. Join a group (either online or off) of like-minded, similarly focused individuals.

* * *

Cultivate the interactions and follow up on conversations. Once you have a few people in your orbit, invite others in.

* * *

This group can become the foundation of your career and some of your dearest friends—but you must make it happen.

* * *

No tribe will form unless someone reaches out to someone else.

Making Things Is a Job

MIKE RUGNETTA,
PRODUCER AND PERFORMER

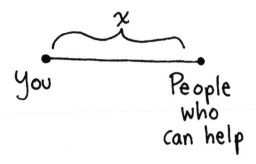

$x = $ Just a few clicks

Hey Mike,

Thanks for offering to hear me out on some of my anxieties. I guess that's what they are? I'd love any advice that pops into your head since it sounds like I'm in a place that you were at a bit ago. Like, where one takes stock of all their accrued expertise and begins to wonder how the hell they might . . . eat. Oh, and seek fulfillment. And also placate those demons which stomp around the head and shoulders, demanding nourishment through creative endeavors. Yeah. You know, that place.

Basically, I'm needing soon to pick some kind of job. Uni is almost over and I'm pretty sure I want to make things, but I have no idea which things, and I'm also kind of worried the pursuit of some of those things isn't exactly fiscally sound. Going back to demons, there are the ravenous, creative ones who tell me to pursue what I love, whatever that may be and whatever the financial risks, and then there is this pragmatic one (probably wearing glasses) who suggests I aim just for monetary return. At some point, it simplifies to a binary "which demon do I listen to" scenario. It's not quite heart versus head, but it's something.

Woe is me, with a problem that no shortage of soon-to-be Formerly Art Students wrestle with! But I'm just feeling so stuck. It's weird that emotions are involved. And that passion for making things. And basically *it's a decision on how to spend my time, but also how to support myself as a functional human who needs to buy things, like food to put in my face. And they tell you to follow your heart, but what does that even mean? And my brain is busy thinking of stupid metaphors about demons and ... help?*

—Jamy

Hey Jamy,

Thanks for the email! I know exactly the feelings you are experiencing, and addressing them is pretty complicated. It's very different for different people. I can tell you what I did, but I also want to be really clear about something: Just because this is what I did doesn't mean it's also what you should do. We all have gut feelings. And our guts are occasionally pretty smart. I guess what I'm saying is, if this email kick-starts a gut feeling, that's awesome; it shouldn't replace one that already exists, though.

So, which shoulder-demons to listen to? One of my old instructors in college gave me a piece of advice. He said, "Do what you love. Money comes later." I took that advice. It was, and remains, the worst piece of advice I've ever received, and the worst piece of advice I've ever taken. I am also very glad I took it. I know that's confusing. Sorry.

I am very lucky. I could afford, for a million reasons (no debt, in-demand technical skills, supportive parents, no dependents, good health, stubbornness, which has got me in trouble in a hundred other situations but was helpful in freelancing) to quit a well-paying but boring-as-shit job to work in the arts and media. I could afford, in the literal sense, to "do what I love" and to wait for the money to "come later." I could live. And be self-sufficient. And happy. And productive. And not worried or stressed about living on the street. At the time I made the transition from "job I hated" to "job I love," I ended up making very little money, but I was making it on things I very much loved doing, and after seven years of hard work I now make a decent living at those same things. This is why I am glad to have taken that advice. Because it worked for me. Not everyone is so lucky. And to be clear, I was lucky.

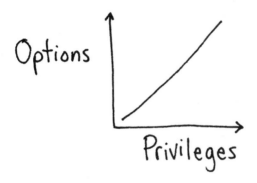

Many people cannot afford to take that advice because they have student debt, because they have a family that requires them to have a well-paying job, or because they have health problems. And so when they hear the advice, "Do what you love. Money comes later!" they feel like if they don't take it, they're giving up. They feel like they're not trying hard enough or that they're not good enough or not sacrificing enough, and if only they really meant it, they could make it and solve all those other (mostly monetary) problems by doing what they love. In my experience, the universe is not so kind to most people. It does not return what you put into it. Or, at the very least, it has no responsibility to do so.

I believe it is true to a certain degree that you can make your own luck by working hard, being talented, making connections, being easy to work with, and so on—we'll talk more about that in a minute—but if your personal situation means that you have to be practical, if it prevents you from going down a road where you'd risk not being able to pay your rent or your medical bills or support your folks, that is not a bad thing. You are not giving up what you love or your destiny or some debt you owe to yourself, the world, whatever.

Too often, especially in professions in which one is making things, we collapse the space between the work and our selves. We confuse what we make with who we are. This is a very, very dangerous thing to do because it robs us of our own agency. It takes the power of being a person away from us and offloads it entirely onto external things that are difficult, costly, impermanent, and subject to so. much. criticism. What's worse is that this kind of forfeiture (or whatever you want to call it) has been romanticized as the base condition of The Artist: the person who cannot rest until the creative force within is exorcised through the Heroic Act of Creation.

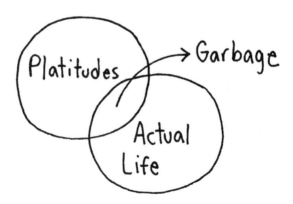

It's a bunch of bullshit. It's an effect of this weird Stay Hungry Narrative and I hate it. It's a shitty cliché that you need to always be hungry, always move up, always work toward the next thing, and always sacrifice your life for that thing. It's a lie. You don't have to. Only dealers, producers, agents, and distributors actually believe this nonsense, and they say it because if creators get content, then they are out of a job. It's a lie that even if you're satisfied with whatever you're currently doing, you should (ʸ °□°)ʸ ︵ ┻━┻ and go out there to pursue some creative endeavor. Just because you flip a table does not mean you're going to end up on some Top 10 list somewhere. It doesn't mean that. You can want something so badly it feels like there is no air in the room, but that doesn't mean you will get it. No amount of work will necessarily result in success. This is especially true in creative fields.

Making things is a job. Sometimes it's a really fun job! But it's never not a job. And the thing that's really hard and weird and disappointing about it is that if you don't treat it the same way you would any other job, you won't be successful. Making things is not some escape from the trappings of Normal Jobness. There are politics, there's social and professional ladder climbing, and there's plotting and scheming. The cast of characters is even the same: There are people who want to see you fail and people with ulterior motives; there are people who will be jealous and people of whom you will be endlessly jealous. A friend of mine, who, after working in production for over ten years, just moved to an office job, said, "It's shocking. There are politics everywhere."

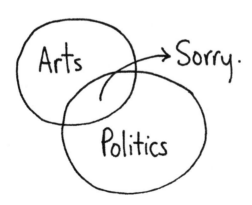

There's a talk by Darius Kazemi that I love. He gave it at XOXO in Portland in 2014. In it, he compares Success™ to winning the lottery. When you make something, you are essentially buying a lottery ticket. That ticket might win. It might not. The more things you make, the more lottery tickets you have purchased. And the more lottery tickets you have, the higher your chances of winning the lottery.

I like this idea because it doesn't sidestep the totally not romantic and rather crushing fact that there is a cost inherent to making things. Making things is costly. Not always in money. And it's not always a significant cost. But it's always costly to some degree. And the more you can afford to "spend," the more likely you are to "win."

It also doesn't sidestep the notion of hope. After playing the lottery hundreds of times without winning, what is going to keep you playing the lottery? For many players of the actual lottery I would guess it's some complicated combination of hope, habit, and boredom that varies with each individual. For many people making things for a living, I would venture to guess that hoping to succeed plays a big part, but they cannot and should not subsist on that hope alone. This is where the metaphor begins to break down.

Darius doesn't talk much about the process of purchasing lottery tickets. Buying a real lottery ticket has a relatively low cost and requires relatively little effort, time, and investment. The cost, time, and effort required for making things, however, is absurd. It is astronomical. It is the reason, in my experience, most people stop making things. Because it is just too hard. It is emotionally draining or physically taxing or economically unsustainable, or any combination of the three.

You have to love the act of making things. You have to love the process of buying your lottery tickets even if they don't bring home the big bucks. You have to love getting your hands dirty and fighting with your creations, and you have to love the challenge of making it happen even if it never sees the light of day or never makes you a buck. And no one might ever say you're a genius or revolutionary or important. You have to love making things sans all the romance of creation and profit. You have to love the process.

That is the "demon to listen to." Not the one that tells you you're going to make it, that if you find the right audience or make something that's good enough, your problems will be solved. Not the one that says if you work harder, every other trouble will take care of itself. Not the one that conflates your self worth with your creative output.

The demon to listen to is the one that encourages you to do something you love when you can find the time to do it responsibly, and then praises you for having exercised that bit of self-care. Listen to the part of you that is terrified to show new work to strangers and try to figure out what you're actually afraid of. Rejection? Self-reflection? Failure? And then listen to the other part of you that knows the point is the process, and as long as the process is enjoyable, everything else is gravy.

This is how you make your own luck. This is how you buy the greatest number of lottery tickets—by following those impulses directed entirely at making things, not the ones concerned with the success or quality of those things. That is how you "make it," because this means any chance you have to create something, anything, is "making it." Success, in my very earnest opinion, is not a place you arrive at; it is a very awkward thing you are constantly learning how to hold on to. If your success is predicated upon doing, as opposed to arriving, you will always be succeeding.

And so, if this arrangement is in any way tenable, if you can feel as though the world does not owe you for your efforts, and if you are personally and responsibly capable of doing so, and if you can do it without romance and without expectation: Do what you love. The money will come later. If you're lucky.

—Mike

Act on This

Tune up your luck engine.

Your luck engine has three parts:

✳ ✳ ✳

1. Your work

Make more, and make better. This takes
time, dedication, and acceptance of the fact that
today's work will suck in comparison to what
you can make next year.

✳ ✳ ✳

2. Your network

Reach out to others, and reply with generosity
when others reach out to you. Your relations are the
foundation of your career, and building a solid foundation
takes a lot of time, a lot of energy, and optimism that
most people are both imperfect and important
in equally unique ways (just like you are).

✳ ✳ ✳

3. Your customers

Work with others in mind. What you create
only matters as much as it can emotionally
affect someone else. Focus on the empathy in your
work, and the attention will come.
If you're lucky.

"What Do You Do?"

EMMA KOENIG,
TELEVISION WRITER AND HUMORIST

It's a deceptively simple question that seems to come up constantly. We're asked this by everyone from the attractive stranger we hope to seduce, to the potential employer we hope to impress, to the rude relative we hope to shut down. (Cool it with the questions, Uncle Steve!) This notion of asking people what they do has come to represent a way to be polite and make socially acceptable small talk.

But it usually doesn't come across that way. In the five to ten years (or more!) after you graduate from college, "What do you do?" can feel ridiculously loaded, largely in part because it feels like you need to distinguish between *what you do* and *how you earn money*. Then there's the trouble of being a freelancer, which inevitably has stretches of terror-ridden unemployment.

I should preface this by saying that I am in the arts/entertainment world, which, like any discipline, has its own particular quirks and rules to breaking in and moving up. Some jobs in this field are only paid in "exposure" and "experience," but others pay so well that it almost feels like there's been some terrible mistake—the Director's Guild minimum for directing an hour of television is $42,701.

Entertainment unions have fairly high minimums to protect us, because you may only get one short-term, well-paying job a year, and you have to figure out how to make that money last. (It also costs thousands to join a union, which is mandatory at a certain point, but that's a story for a different day, kids!)

In any case, pursuing work in this industry requires a slightly different kind of hustle than say, trying to rise in the finance world. And I know nothing about that world besides watching *The Wolf of Wall Street* and loving every second of it. But this is all just a roundabout way of saying that the following is fairly artist-specific.

At the moment, I am a TV writer for a new romantic comedy on ABC. It's pretty much the first time in my post-college career that I've been able to succinctly describe what I do.

"I'm a TV writer."

I can say it without over-explaining, providing disclaimers, or rambling on until the person I'm talking to cuts me off. It's the first time that what I do aligns with my full-time job. But it was not always this way.

The Prep

I graduated from college with a BFA in Drama, which I know does not sound like the most economically viable career path. There is a built-in struggle inherent with pursuing a life in the arts, so I knew the jobs weren't going to start lining up for me right away. But despite this, I truly believed that I was supposed to be working in the entertainment industry. I'll get to that a little later.

I graduated a semester early from college, saving enough to have a little cushion in paying the rent. Part of the reason I was able to graduate early was because of certain credits I'd earned through AP classes in high school. So essentially, my work ethic as a sixteen-year-old ended up helping me as a twenty-two-year-old.

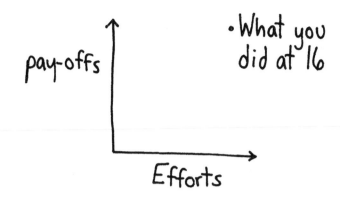

In fact, a lot of decisions I made as a teenager led me toward admittance to the college I wanted and getting the training in my desired field. It's scary as hell to think that your adolescent decisions can have repercussions for decades, but it's also kind of thrilling. Since I've always known I wanted to be in entertainment, I prepared for that accordingly as a kid.

Despite this preparation, my career took some unexpected turns. If you had asked me a few years ago to predict what I'd be doing professionally, I would have had no idea I'd become an author and not an actor. But I think you have to get as good as you can for the job you want, and then expect your five-year plan to keep evolving beyond that job.

I have tried to be open to every facet of the industry I wanted to be part of, because sometimes you have to go through the doors that are open to be able to get the keys to the doors that are locked. Whoa, is that confusing self-help imagery or what? But you get what I'm saying, right?

The Daydream

My first job out of school was as a coat check girl. Believe me, it was far from glamorous. It's incredible to go from graduating college to getting yelled at for hanging up coats wrong. I didn't even know there was a "wrong" way to hang up coats.

I was getting paid only in tips, so I was not raking it in. It was typically around $150 a night, but I only worked there a few nights a week. In between hanging up coats and getting chastised, I wasn't allowed to read a book or look at my phone or talk to anyone. I was basically sitting in a chair staring into space for seven hours. It gave me a lot of time to daydream.

Speaking of daydreaming, I also worked behind the counter of a sandwich shop and had to stand for hours on end. I would let my mind drift. I would doodle on the butcher paper we used to wrap up the sandwiches.

At one point, I interned at a production company. In the downtime between data entry and coffee runs, I outlined ideas I wanted to develop art pieces about.

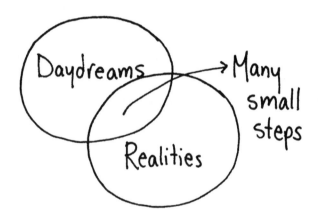

Basically, in every job I've had where I've been bored out of my mind, I tried to use that time wisely. I let my mind wander to the things I wanted to write and create. I thought about my career goals. I focused on what my priorities were.

Without even realizing it, I was giving myself the time to meditate on what was important to me. Obviously, you don't want this to impair your ability to do your job, but I am a big advocate for daydreaming.

We shove so much content into our brains, we usually don't give our-selves sufficient time to foster original thoughts.

For example, I happen to love listening to podcasts while walking (and have developed an immeasurable crush on Marc Maron), but I find it important to take the headphones off sometimes and force myself to be alone with my thoughts.

When you give up external stimulation for a minute, your brain is forced to stimulate itself! (Get your minds out of the gutter!) That is exactly when you are going to have your amazing idea. That is when you are going to decide you want to try something new. That is when you are going to talk yourself into doing something you're afraid of.

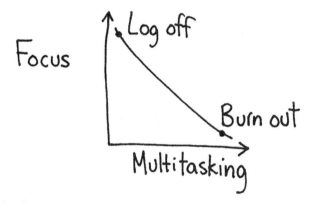

Half-reading a BuzzFeed article, while half-watching reality TV, while half-listening to a ukulele cover of a hip hop song, while half Gchatting with your friend from high school may be an impressive dis-play of multitasking, but I doubt that your brain is going to stumble upon your next great idea that way.

All of my daydreaming led me to create these little drawings about what I was going through, which ended up changing the course of my life. These drawings ended up leading to a larger art project online, which then became a book, which was in development to be a TV show. Which is totally insane.

So I guess what I'm saying is that even when you're freaking out the most, you need to carve out a little time to let your subconscious work its magic and lead you to your next professional strategy.

Finding the Joy

It seems counterintuitive, but a lot of the things that have helped move my career forward have been the things that I did to feel personally fulfilled.

I like to think about projects passing the "Bedroom Test," as in, could I spend hours and hours working on this alone in my bedroom and still feel motivated and excited by it? If I never showed this to anyone, would it still make me happy? Getting to share your art with others can be the greatest feeling ever, but ideally, you should be so passionate about whatever you're creating that you can derive joy just from *your* experience with it. Things that pass the Bedroom Test often become the pieces that people connect with the most.

Having said that, don't confuse process with product. It's rarely fun and easy the entire time you are creating something, but it's important to take stock of your creative process so you can start to discern the difference between a project that feels challenging but fulfilling, and a project that feels impossible and painful.

Also, it's easier said than done to focus on the things you're passionate about while you're trying to make enough money to survive. I know. I literally wrote the book (*F*ck! I'm in My Twenties*) on how frustrating that part of my life was.

But I was always working on something creative for myself while I had other jobs, and I tried to be as disciplined as possible. I would come home from an irksome job and dive right into working on something. That doesn't mean it wasn't tiring or annoying. That doesn't mean my mind didn't go to some dark places.

But my solution has always been to talk about what you're going through with other people, because that is where you're going to get the reminder that you're not alone and feel recharged enough to keep hustling.

The Belief

No one cares about your career more than you do. No one. And if there is someone who puts more mental energy into thinking about your career than you, that is a problem. Even if you have help, even if you have a mentor, at the end of the day, you are the president and CEO of your own business. You have to take charge.

I'm not really a religious person, but as I struggled with getting work post-college, I started to understand the point of it. When you're trying to get your foot in the door, you have to constantly remind yourself to believe in something you can't yet see: yourself, as a thriving, successful person.

After I got my book deal, I was able to get representation, something I'd been chasing for years. I thought it was going to be smooth sailing now that I finally had a team, but I found that it wasn't a magic tool to suddenly get everything I wanted.

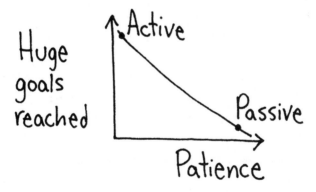

It was my own *impatience* about my career that pushed things forward. I wanted things to happen quickly, so I took things into my own hands. Yes, it is essential to find satisfaction at every level, but if you get too satisfied, too comfortable, there is not going to be a lot of movement in your career.

I went out to LA to try to sell a TV show based on my book. I had no specific training in this, but I believed that I could figure it out. I read a ton of how-to books and scripts and tried to prepare as much as possible. I went to a lot of general meetings, which are essentially like job interviews for jobs that don't exist yet, and where you also get a free water bottle.

I was in a new city where I barely knew anybody and didn't have a car or a clue, but I had a really clear goal. It was the combination of the support of the people around me (including the generosity of my boyfriend at the time, who let me crash at his place for months while I took this intense financial gamble) and my own stubbornness about my career that eventually led me to the finish line. Within ten months of my arrival, I had sold my show to NBC.

If I had let it sink in how difficult my goal was or if I had expected other people to do all the work for me, it wouldn't have happened. I had to keep believing in a version of me that didn't exist yet.

The Highs and Lows

Between the book and the TV show, I had a big year and then . . . it was radio silence, er, television silence.

The TV show never got made. I wrote something new that I was really excited about, and it went nowhere. I started a lot of things I couldn't finish. I started to wonder if I would ever have a good idea again.

I spent the following year doing weekly cartoons for a British newspaper. I cried a lot. I put out another book. But despite the cartoons and some sporadic freelance positions, I was starting to run out of money.

I started to doubt myself a lot. I started to get very anxious and wonder if I would have to take another restaurant job. But I jumped back into discipline. I drew up elaborate charts of goals I wanted to accomplish and different tasks I needed to get done each day. I started waking up early and writing alongside a friend every morning. I kept going to meetings and trying to make things happen. And after about two years of recalibrating and chugging along, my luck changed.

In the knick of time, I got hired to write for a TV show. Suddenly I had to move across the country again.

I know the career I have chosen will probably never be steady, and I will most likely always be worried about money, but I try to look at the average of what I've done. I spend some days in my pajamas surfing the Internet and fearfully wondering what my next move will be, and some days I get to go to an awesome job in my industry. The reality of my career lives somewhere in between.

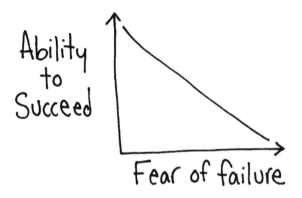

In a couple of weeks, this TV show could get canceled and I will be unemployed again, back to searching for the next answer to "What do you do?" and for the next way to earn money. But I have experienced the rise and fall before, and I know I can do it again.

Act on This

Write down the four biggest things
you've done (accidentally or purposefully) in the
last six years.

* * *

Now, noodle out how those capabilities can
translate into different kinds of day-to-day work.

* * *

Take your time, give yourself creative
liberties with job titles, and think as far beyond a
résumé as you can.

Start the Conversation You Want to Have

ASHA DORNFEST,
FOUNDER OF *PARENT HACKS*

You're not alone. You're not too late. You can do it (whatever *it* is).

It's not empty cheerleading to say these things. I know because I did it (whatever *it* is) myself, and I see other people doing it every day, right now. Writing books. Selling art. Developing apps. Teaching workshops. Becoming celebrities. Changing opinions. Starting movements.

The Internet is many things, and will be many more things by the time this book hits the shelves/screens, but it will *always* be fertile ground for connection—real, breathing humans sharing ideas with other real, breathing humans, which is where all good things begin to grow.

In 2005, I started a blog. By now, you've probably heard a hundred stories that start with this line. But it's important for me to start here so you have context for what comes next.

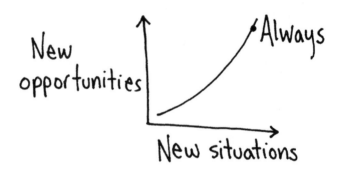

I'd already been a writer for many years, but I was a relatively new parent and I was reeling from it, utterly disoriented by my new life. My description of early parenthood sounds overdramatic, but I can't seem to find more accurate words.

I started *Parent Hacks* as a way to share practical tips for simplifying life with young kids. I wasn't an expert in such tips—I needed them *myself*. Starting a blog wasn't a strategic decision nor was it a career move. It was a cry for help. I figured that if someone had a good idea, I could pass it on. If I shared enough good ideas, perhaps it might help other new parents.

Like most pivotal moments, I had no idea at the time that this was mine.

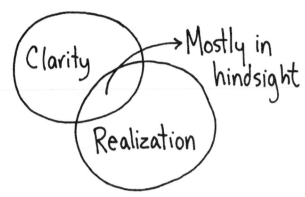

Within six months I found myself with a thriving community of readers, contributors, and colleagues. The following years brought opportunities to write, speak, and travel, along with a network of friends all over the country.

But that's the sparkly part. Nobody's career is a straight arrow pointing to the stars. There have been bad decisions, broken commitments, and periods of insecurity and self-doubt. Home life grew more complicated as my kids got older, and there were months when my work retreated into the shadowy corners. Sometimes I would disappear from the Internet entirely, without notice.

And yet, I was never alone. For me, "starting a blog" wasn't just starting a blog—it was the beginning of a conversation that bolstered me when I could barely respond with a weak "thank you." It also continues to sustain me today as my oldest child strides off to high school.

My blog's origin story has an obnoxiously Golden Ticket aura about it. Success came quickly, without much effort or planning. I'm not saying I haven't earned it—I'm a good writer and a decent human, and I had enough chutzpah to proclaim my idea worthy of other people's attention—but timing and luck played a crucial part in my initial success, arguably *the* most crucial part.

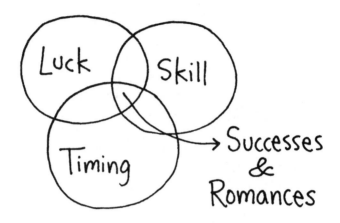

The thing about quick success is that it can't last, at least not in its initial form. Making a real go of it takes persistence. And therein lies the secret of my hustle, the quieter, less glamorous months and years that followed the early salad days of my blog. The part where I kept going after the initial flash bulbs faded, and I had to rely on the light of my own candle flicker to see my way forward.

The narrative would bore you to tears, so rather than dragging you along the switchbacks of what I've been doing for the last ten years, let me instead share what I've learned.

It's all been said and done before. But not by YOU.

The worry that your big idea isn't big enough or original enough or special enough can stop you right out of the gate. Smarter, more talented, better-funded people than you have already done it before. In fact, they might be doing it *right now*. What chance could you possibly have?

You have the same chance I had when I launched a website with no plan beyond "write" and "help" to an audience of zero, at a time when few parents had even heard of blogs.

I believed I had something of value to contribute even though my idea wasn't entirely new—I certainly didn't invent parenting tips. But I suspected I wasn't alone in feeling let down by the expert advice in the parenting magazines I pored over every month. And I wanted to do something about it. So I did.

I placed myself in the path of the lucky lightning bolt, should it happen to strike.

Work harder, not smarter.

For many, confidence isn't the problem; overanalyzing is. Believe me, I know. I'm a lifelong overanalyzer (ask my friends).

Does this sound familiar? Before you can even get started, you need the perfect business plan or outline or software setup. You need better connections and the right social media profiles and a sound strategy. You need to work smarter, not harder. Right? Wrong.

Internet hustlers begin by working harder. A *lot* harder, for a lot longer than you think. It's only in the hard work that you become smarter.

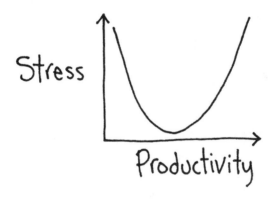

A growing portfolio of work, even imperfect work, is a hundred times more valuable than a "proven" strategy and 100,000 followers.

Connection before perfection.

The Internet may seem like a cyberworld wired together by code and fueled by algorithms, but it's actually a simple framework built to support the most basic of human needs: connection.

Your audience is your *ally*. When you deliver thoughtful, honest work, week after week, month after month, your audience not only grows, but the people in it also look past your work and come to trust you.

Never forget: Trust, more than anything else, is your metric for success. When you have the trust of your audience, they will move and grow with you. They will root for you when you try something new.

They will support you as your interests change, and they will wait if you need to step away for a time.

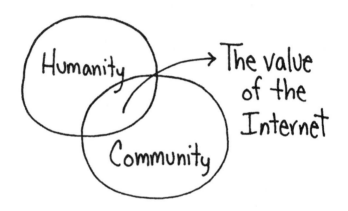

It's all too easy to be seduced into "crafting your social media strategy" and "optimizing your content for viral sharing," but in so doing, your audience ceases to be the living, breathing humans they are, and instead they just become numbers. I don't trust anyone who treats me like a number. And neither will they.

I've fallen into this trap myself. The more distracted I was by my strategy, the further I drifted from the work that earned me an audience in the first place.

I found myself cranking out material that was easy to digest, but lacking in substance. I gradually went from feeling like a contributing member of a vital community to a burnt-out production worker. It took time and humility for me to admit that some of my own choices got me there.

I'm not suggesting you fly by the seat of your pants, abandoning any attempt to influence your trajectory. I'm reminding you that maintaining and growing your audience starts by seeing the people as people, not as statistics. In return, they'll see you as a person, not a product.

Forget the money for as long as you can.

Part of the driving need to plan and strategize is the fear that there's no money in it if you don't.

Fair enough. You're looking to start a business or create an income. No matter how good trust feels, it doesn't pay the bills.

Except it does. Which is to say, trust is the foundation on which paying customers stand.

Tempting as it is to quit the boring day job and throw your lot in with the hustlers, doing so may actually short-circuit your progress.

The longer your livelihood depends on a different source, the more risk you can take with your creative work and the more time you have to build a connection with your audience based on trust rather than a desire to sell. Think of your day job (or well-employed partner) as a patron of the arts, taking care of the groceries and the phone bill so you can focus on your creative dream.

Oddly enough, the time constraint may actually *increase* your creativity. The less time to fret and "research" (read: procrastinate), the more work you'll get done.

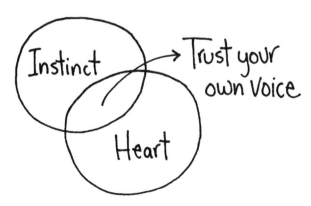

I come to these lessons as a writer, but they're relevant to anyone who dreams of offering something of themselves to the world. Because, really, isn't that what creative entrepreneurship is at its heart? Sure, we hope there's some recognition and money down the line, but that spark, that urge to make something and present it to the world is a fundamentally generous one.

Go. Start that conversation. It's your time to shine.

Act on This

Play 20 questions with yourself: ask things that
have complex (or multiple) answers.

*** * ***

Investigate things that puzzle or confound you,
things that fascinate or flummox you.

*** * ***

Share your answers with someone,
and ask them the same questions.

*** * ***

You'll begin a conversation on topics that
matter and uncover things you need to know.

Bitch. Boss. Boy.

KELSEY HANSON,
FOUNDER OF VOCAL DESIGN

I use these three terms with a smile, and can't believe they're going into a book. They're my mantra—words for being confident, positive, and unafraid. They are the three ways I've always acted that have gotten me into trouble, but have also been drivers of my successes, and they're the basis of my self-understanding.

I have always been bossy, which is not always a good thing, but if you can pull it off with a certain intonation in your voice, they all call you "natural leader" instead of "bossy little thing." I have also always been kind of a tomboy, or really, just more like a boy. Lastly, I'm a bit of a bitch. And no, I'm not vicious or devious. I'm just assertive.

Sometimes, you need to be a bitch.

I'm not trying to encourage you to start fights on the street or throw drinks in someone's face or become a bully. That's gross. By "be a bitch," I mean exude confidence. If you lack it, think hard on why. Go find that problem, seek it out, and solve it. It's OK to be confident in yourself first and say, *I got this*. Confidence is often mistaken for bitchiness. If that's the case, I'll take it. I'd rather be perceived as a bitch than a doormat.

I am constantly competing with whoever is winning. I want to be wearing that #1 trucker hat from the old Will Ferrell sketch, no matter whose house I'm in. I want to be the best at whatever I'm doing. I'm not ashamed of that. I'm not shy about discussing my efforts or skills, I'm not self-deprecating or passive, and yeah, I have been known to brag when I rock. Some people call that bitchy, but I prefer to think of it as manifesting confidence.

For all the success women have had as a gender, I feel like there are some fundamental beliefs still ingrained that we need to question, if not entirely destroy. And a majorly held belief is that women who speak up are bitches, in the most ungenerous usage of the word.

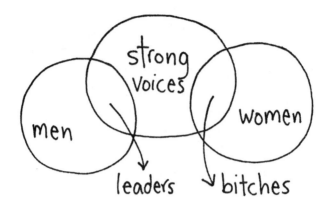

I was in a meeting recently with about eight other people. Most of them were older than me, with higher titles, and half of them were men. I walked in and waited for five minutes, through silence, feet shuffling, and phone checking. Then, I figured it was time to get things moving. I outlined why we were meeting, our objective, and my opinion of what we needed to do. I asked someone else what he thought. The meeting continued from there, like a typical meeting.

As I was leaving, I heard one of the guys say to another, "Scary." SCARY. Because I started a meeting? Is it scary when a man starts a meeting? Nope, that's just par for the course. Well it's time to start meetings, because the only way everyone is going to get used to women leading is if we do it. A LOT. So find your confidence, and take charge.

They might think you are scary (which is work-friendly code for bitchy, anyway) at first. But the time after that? They will give you the floor. They will put you on the email first. They will come to you for answers. They will start respecting you as someone who is trying to get shit done. And the faster you can break those misperceptions, the better.

Sometimes, you need to be a boss.

I've had a lot of bosses. My parents had me out the door working at age fifteen, during summers at least. I've been a babysitter, a receptionist, a hostess, a drive-thru girl at Dairy Queen, a cocktail waitress, and a camp counselor. When I was younger, the jobs were short-term. A job was a job. The boss was the boss. I worked hard and had good work friends. I learned how to strive, to accomplish, to forge relationships with higher-ups, to keep customers happy, and so on.

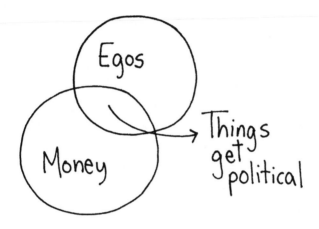

My first *real* boss at my first *real* job taught me a lot about power, politics, and performance. I worked to prove my value to him, and I learned everything I could about the job. As soon as a manager role was open, I marched into his office and basically just assumed the role. I didn't leave him room to say no.

When I first became a boss, I managed a couple of designers on a small in-house creative team. And I was immediately thrown into heady situations. A new-hire designer was rather seriously sexually harassed by an executive. He was forced out, and I had to assume some of his role in the interim. I learned about the HR process and legal lingo. I sat at the table on behalf of the department in huge meetings. I wrote company-wide media plans. I managed contacts and key business relationships. And I acted like I could effortlessly handle it all, along with my normal duties in my role as a designer. I was twenty-five.

After a couple of years, I moved on. I freelanced as an art director. I drank a lot at parties and tried to network, but I needed more experience. So I took a job in an in-house creative group, where I met my first in a chain of eight managers in six years.

The first manager hired me on the spot, and the next week was laid off with a big group. The next one left the country for a fiancé, leaving me with a national product launch at eight months pregnant with my daughter. After that there was a manager who was so bad at managing that he was demoted and quit. I had a manager who was great, but I had to fight like hell to get on his team. Then there was a big reshuffling of people in the name of global business, and I was moved onto the team of yet another boss. This one seemed like a better politician than Ronald Reagan, but turned out to just be a bad actor. I learned a lot from each of them, and the bad examples taught me the most.

I've learned that good bosses are people who hire people who are better than they are, and are confident enough to not be afraid and to be constantly improving themselves. They support, coach, and have your back. They have ways of quietly proving to you that there are reasons they are in charge. A good boss is like a good teacher, or a good military leader, or a great parent. They empower you, because they know that in the end everyone will benefit. They take the time to hire good people and put good leaders in place. The bottom line will reflect it. Do everyone a favor and hire good leaders, everywhere.

Now that I'm a CEO and my own boss, I finally get to act like one. Brazenly assuming responsibility is dangerous to do in corporate culture, but it's mandatory out here in the independent world. And it's exhilarating and overwhelming all at once.

Every day, I remember what I always wanted and needed and loved and hated in a boss. And informed by my experience, I try to be the best boss to the people who have trusted me with that role, because I don't want to be just any boss, I want to be a great one.

Sometimes, you need to be a boy.

I am the oldest of three girls. There were no boys, so I spent a lot of time being treated like a boy. I think this treatment is common among first-born kids, to be treated with more rules and higher standards.

I went fishing with my dad. I helped him build cabins. We watched Husky games. We played catch. I went to his office and drew with his markers. I played sports, and that's all we talked about. We're all conditioned to fit into rigid gender roles, and the truth is, none of us fit exactly. The boyish side of me is an asset, and here's why:

Hanging out with boys was always a learning experience for me. I learned how to build fires in the woods and on the beach. I learned how to drive a stick shift at age fourteen. And a boat. And a dirt bike. I learned about football and how to golf and have good golf etiquette, and about underground rap from the Bay area. I took my Blazer 4-bying. I went camping in the snow. I took crazy hikes with backpacks full of beer. I drank Everclear in Montana, took last-minute road trips, floated rivers, ate chicken-fried steak, played pool and poker, and tried chewing Copenhagen (nasty).

I learned how to shotgun beers, and compression-start my car, and make a sparkler bomb, and that a firm handshake is important, and that knowledge of any inland waterways, tides, and fishing seasons is important for small talk.

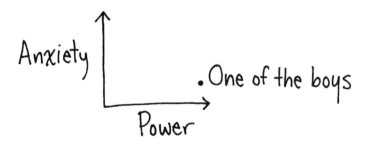

Boys (and men; you know, large boys) can bullshit casually. They can find commonality without drama. They can separate business and personal relationships, and then blur that line on the golf course, and then write the whole thing off as an expense with zero guilt.

When things go south, boys try again. They have more resilience and a competitive nature, maybe because they aren't obsessed with details and what everyone else thinks. They have room in their head-space to think about ideas. They've been raised to have that space. The culture is built for them to be in charge. And women need to learn how to think like they do, to assume more power and freedom and to assert themselves like the boys do. They should draft off of their leads, because it will help break down the invisible walls between them all in the boardroom, to be "one of the boys." Like it or not, it's still important to be one of the boys.

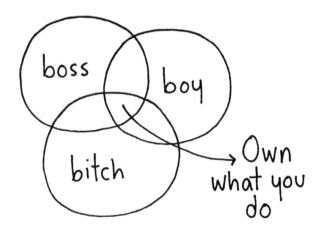

Be a bitch. Assert yourself and you'll be respected.
Be a boss. Be a leader you can respect.
Be a boy. Act like you belong where you want to be.

Act on This

Carefully choose three words that describe you—this is the shortest autobiography you will ever write.

* * *

Make sure they are all very different from each other (no synonyms; that's cheating). Consider how you present yourself in relation to these three words.

* * *

Which one of these words do you use as a mask? Which one is your truest self?

* * *

Which one is something you try to pass as?

* * *

Are your chosen words crutches or pedestals?

* * *

And finally, ask yourself, "Are these the words I want to live with, or replace with a new vocabulary or identity?"

Let Your Inner Child OUT

MÓNICA GUZMÁN,
COLUMNIST AND NEIMAN FELLOW

I do my best writing groggy, with bad breath.

It's ugly. As a kid I imagined a cozy writing nook, a warm cup of tea and, I don't know, sunlight streaming through the windows.

Instead, I go from bed to our low black sofa with the lights off, happy no one could possibly see my ratty hair and too-big nightshirt. I sit on the far end, settle under a gray fleece blanket, open my eleven-inch MacBook Air with my face turned away—the light is a shocker at five in the morning—and type. This is journalism at its most glamorous.

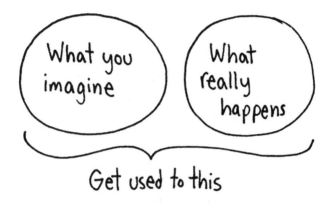

There's a reason this works. This early in the morning, with this little activity, my creative mind is fresh but my self-doubting mind is not. I've learned, over time, that the more I get out while I'm too tired to nitpick, while the echoes of crazy dreams still bounce around in my head, the more interesting my final work will be.

Theoretically speaking, my ugly mornings ensure that I think like a Child.

In an application of psychologist Eric Berne's "Parent/Adult/Child" theory, author and writing coach Dinty W. Moore argues that writers have three modes of thinking: the playful Child, the questioning Adult, and the critical Parent. The trick is in knowing when to apply each. "When you begin a project, begin it with the Child attitude, pushing words around on the page . . . just to see what develops," he writes.

"Allowing the Parent voice to enter into the process too soon . . . can shut down the enterprise entirely."

Moore is talking about writing, but this Child/Parent model works in life, too—especially the free-ranging creative one. It gives you a way to think through a big paradox at the heart of every hustle: how to lead yourself while getting out of your own way.

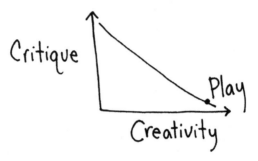

Some people *shakes fist* strike this happy balance from the start. I was an anxious student, an approval-seeking employee. I interviewed Seattle's inspiringly bold geeks for years and envied what they could do. The Parent ruled my life and I knew it.

Then in 2012, less than a year after I became a freelance journalist, I gave birth to my son.

Toddlers are about as free-range creative as humans get. They don't need to manage their critical voices. The "Child" attitude is the only one they've got.

They're wholly unprepared for the world (obviously), but they have us adults beat on one thing: They are at every moment, for better or worse, completely and unquestionably *themselves*.

Ralph Waldo Emerson, whose essay "Self-Reliance" I play in my car when I feel weak, calls the shameless confidence with which a little boy judges the world the "healthy attitude of human nature."

"He cumbers himself never about consequences, about interests: He gives an independent, genuine verdict," Emerson said. "You must court him: He does not court you."

My son is giving me the biggest time-management challenges I'll ever face. But he's inspiring me to work smarter. Acting like a toddler is a terrible idea. But letting myself think like one, when appropriate, gives me these crystal-clear glances into what I like, and what I want to do.

Why bother to work for myself if I don't get to have any fun? Adults "work." Children "play." I think the kids are onto something.

For Christmas, my parents got my son a microphone. It was a perfect gift and an obvious one: Ever since we started showing him YouTube videos of our favorite rock classics he's been dancing across the living room, crooning into whatever's around to anyone who will listen. And even anyone who won't.

Wonder → Tinker → Know (cycle) } Why playtime is valuable

But the thing is, there were no bad gifts to my son this Christmas. He's a kid. Everything he does reveals what he loves, and the adults who want him to prosper can't help but pay attention.

When I begin my work with a period of play as shameless as my son's wails into the toilet plunger, I tend to like the result.

But it isn't easy. Toddlers' free play is endorsed by the world; the best playrooms have tons of toys and no agendas. We adults are terrified of play. We don't always know what we want to play with. And when we do, we're afraid it isn't cool enough. Familiar enough. Important enough. We're afraid that it won't result in enough measurable gains for ourselves, or make enough sense to anybody else.

Adults know, more or less, how to structure kids' play for minimum harm and maximum benefit. But we have no idea how to do it for ourselves.

Working is easy. It's *playing* that's hard.

I can think of several times when channeling my inner Child—and committing to her transparent, playful interests—led directly to work I'm proud of. I wrote one tech column for the *Seattle Times* entirely as a series of provocative questions after reading Padgett Powell's "Interrogative Mood" and experimenting with the form.

In another column, I took on questions about the personal impact of so much digital writing by penning absolutely every digital communication I sent over two days—email, tweet, text—by hand.

But I'm a writer. When I play with something unfamiliar to me, something exciting but risky, keeping my inner Parent away gets especially tricky.

After I covered a vlogging conference a couple years back, all I wanted to do was experiment with video, so I summoned my Child and started posting personal videos on my feeds. They weren't perfect and they weren't what people expected, but for several magical weeks I didn't care. I was learning tons about production, storytelling, and most importantly, sharpening my sense for what's interesting. Oh, and I was having *fun*.

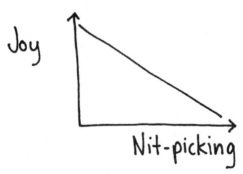

Then two people I know told me my videos weren't their thing, and my inner Parent broke through. What am I doing? Do my videos suck? They didn't, but it didn't matter: Playtime was over, earlier than it should have been. Good parents don't question their toddlers' play. They also know better than to mess with their rhythms.

I work most efficiently in the morning, and I've wasted countless hours of my working life not bothering to notice that. I used to save my undone work for the end of the day. It seemed a natural choice: Tack on bonus tasks to those last, bonus hours. I'd stare at the screen, and stare at it, and stare at it, yawn, and blame my lack of productivity on a lack of motivation. It was idiotic.

Usually, when our son acts up, gets moody, or enters what we call his "no" mood, it's not because he wants to. It's because he's tired. Toddler energy levels are everything, it turns out, and honoring your particular kid's particular rhythms is Parenting 101.

Their kid naps at 11 a.m., yours at 2 p.m., and you're going to miss each other at this other kid's party. No one minds: Why show up with your kid when he'll barely show up himself?

We adults have our rhythms, too, and being a free-range creative means never having to caffeine your way through a silly 9 to 5 ever again. But there's little point in escaping these default schedules if you don't optimize your work around your own rhythm.

So the ugly mornings will continue. My inner Child will have it no other way.

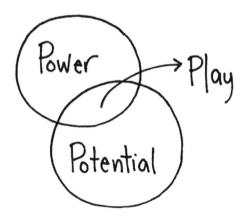

Act on This

Carve out a chunk of time every day (or week) for yourself—before work, after work, on a weekend, whenever makes the most sense for YOU.

✱ ✱ ✱

Allow yourself to think thoughts and make things during your creative time, in your creative space, free from digital, social, or work-related interruptions. Too much structure can prevent creativity from happening.

Do the Math

THOMAS LEVERITT,
DIRECTOR, AUTHOR, AND PAINTER

OK, the first thing to understand about being a freelancer is that you're going into business. You are therefore a capitalist. You may not want to be, but here you are. Sucks to be you.

Therefore, you need a very clear idea of what you are trying to do with your life. However you plan to get by, you need a bigger goal that you're working toward. "Make rent" will not cut it anymore.

Money

When I came out of school at age eighteen, I just set off running, doing things. I figured if I did them well enough, money would magically stick to me. And it's true, it sort of does. But I really wish someone had sat me down and laid out the birds and bees of money.

There are two ways to make money: labor and capital. Labor means you put in an honest day's work, whether it's laying bricks or dispensing legal advice, and you get paid for that work. Capital means you already have money, and *that* money earns money. That can be interest on cash, or dividends from stocks or bonds. Income from capital is really the way to go, because you literally don't do anything and you get paid anyway. Living entirely off interest and dividends is called being rich, or retired.

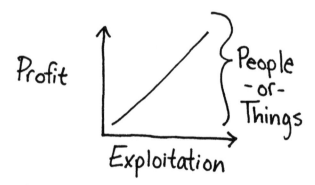

This brings us to your mission in life: to go from living on 100 percent labor and 0 percent capital, to 0 percent labor and 100 percent capital. There are other forms of income, like state pensions and social security, if they even exist by the time you retire, but best not to rely on those. Let all of that be a pleasant surprise. But retirement will not be something that magically happens to you at sixty-five. It's something you have to work toward every day of your life.

Now, most people are idiots, so their retirement has to be taken out of their control, through things like company 401(k)s. Going freelance includes the implicit declaration: I'm adult enough to manage all that myself.

But are you?! A crucial metric of how well you're freelancing is how well you're progressing with your money. But it's not the only metric. There are others, like: Do you despise the very fabric of your days? And, are you an asshole? But it's a super important question, and one I constantly see freelancers completely ignore.

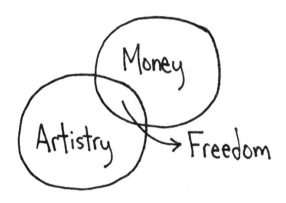

When I was in college, I spent a ton of money on books. I bought a lot, I read a lot, I amassed a house full of 'em. It brought me a lot of pleasure. But that seems vaguely naïve now. What retirement looks like to me is not a library of books, but of small virtual devices that produce 4 percent income per year. If instead of books (which are a pretty twentieth-century affectation at this point anyway), you collected income-producing securities, you slowly bring forward the day when you are not living gig-to-gig. Let's say Treasuries are getting 4 percent, and you reckon you can live as an old codger on $40,000 a year, then all you need to do is save up a million bucks. Get going.

You need to know where you are on this road. If you look at these numbers and think, *Holy fuck, there's no way I'll make it,* then get the hell off the road and get a job with 401(k) contributions. If you think you can make it, (A) welcome, and (B) I like the fight in you, kid, and (C) keeping an eye on your capital income means that you will sleep one entire fuck of a lot better.

NB: Don't be an asshole capitalist. Don't invest in companies that pollute egregiously, make weapons, or fund people and programs that go against your moral code.

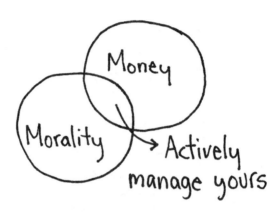

NB: America taxes income from labor (income tax) at up to 40 percent, and income from capital (capital gains) at 15 percent. So don't let anyone tell you that America values hard work. It actually penalizes hard work and smiles on dividends.

NB: In America, the Self-Employed retirement account (SEP-IRA) allows you to allocate up to $53,000, before tax, toward your retirement account (twice, actually, if you've incorporated your freelance business as a separate entity). That's plenty. Do it.

Do your bookkeeping in Google Spreadsheets. Enter everything you spend, the day, or at least the week, you spend it. Enter everything you're paid, too. This is the place to keep a record of everything you're expecting to bring in, and when and how much you've invoiced people for. Unpaid and late invoices are the perpetual ball-aches of being a freelancer, and you need to be all over who owes you what.

Take the time to put together a virtual tax return so you can see what kinds of things you can claim as expenses, and keep an eye out for those things as you go through your year. You can't run a business if you don't know this stuff. For example, health insurance: There's no reason not to spend money on a reasonable plan, as you can deduct your premiums straight off your tax liability. These are important, no-brainer life decisions, and if you're not all over them like white on rice, you have no business pretending to be an adult. Go back inside.

All these things will have a massive impact on your ability to manage your anxiety.

Anxiety

I addressed money first, but anxiety is probably the most important currency in freelance life. There's literally no point being free of the bullshit and indignities of corporate life if you're too worried about your life to sleep well, exercise, not smoke, or take four-day weekends with a clean conscience when you damn well want. In other words: to enjoy your life.

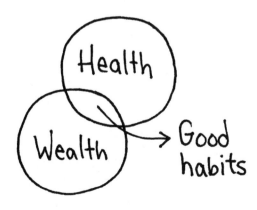

I basically take the view that the human body has evolved to work correctly. Sure, now that we live way longer, we have to take extra care of ourselves with things like toothpaste and yoga, or our teeth and spines will deteriorate before we're ready, but you should be paying attention to your body's warning lights.

What this means is that if you are so anxious or unhappy that you have to put tape over the warning lights with psychotropic drugs just to function like a person, then freelancing might not be for you.

Find some hobbies or something that will help manage your anxiety. For me, that includes swimming, running, keeping my finances on track, and getting up early after eight hours of good sleep. Find what works for you.

Booking Work

This is the hard part: Being a top-gun video journalist or children's entertainer is worthless unless you can also make money walk in the door. Entire TV series revolve around the gross contortions people get into to make and retain sales. And one way to get that money is by participating in the orgy of hustlers feigning friendship with other people who might be useful to them. But that's how it's done: Go to parties, meet people, impress them with wit or charm or sex, and if you like each other when the smoke clears, maybe they'll give you some business. In America, everything is business. Keep your receipts.

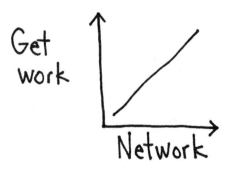

Sell-Side and Buy-Side

The way I see it, the best way to develop a portfolio of clients is first to work on the other side of the fence. Example: You want to be a freelance writer. Head to New York City and rent the cheapest digs you can stand. Spend a few years as a staff writer for *Vice*, Hearst, Condé Nast, BuzzFeed, HuffPo, Thrillist, or any combination thereof. Go to parties. Meet everyone. Throw yourself at Twitter like it's your job (it is). Slowly you'll figure out who the right commissioning editors are, and they'll figure out you're a legit person to hire. Most staff writing jobs will allow you to write elsewhere, so in this case you can incubate a freelance career from the comfort of an admittedly shit salary.

Eventually, if you know what you're doing, *National Geographic* will consider you worth sending to the Congo at four bucks a word, and you're there. You can always go back and take a staff job for a while, if it all gets to be more stressful than rewarding.

Prosper

Once you've got the emotional and financial structure in place, it's there to facilitate one of three possible life plans:

1. Make money
2. Be happy
3. Change the world in some way

You need to figure out which one, or which mix you're going for. Most people get spat off the higher-education conveyor belt and rather joylessly go about pursuing #1, and not even that well. Plenty of people—most activists, for example—are miserable and poor but still choose #3, as they literally cannot rest until they see justice done. Freelancers tend to have a pretty big quotient of #2, if for no other reason than they're prickly and difficult people who resent taking direction from morons.

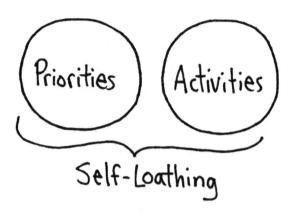

Overall, committing to a life outside the sensory deprivation tank of corporate America is difficult, cold, nerve-racking, and fraught with peril. But it's also kind of great, because it means you get to be present for your own life. So do your math, and you'll stay sane and in the black.

Act on This

Fire up a spreadsheet and ask yourself the hard questions. Look at your finances. Where are you now, and where do you want to be?

✳ ✳ ✳

You don't need to solve everything with this spreadsheet; just create a place where you can be honest with yourself going forward about what money comes in, what goes out, and what you are hanging on to.

Making It Work: Staying Power

CASEY BOWERS, MERCENARY WRITER

Right now, someone somewhere much smarter and savvier than I am (probably younger, too) is writing a book with a title like *Overcoming Ohio*, with the hopes that it will be the triumphant coming-of-age tale of woe and survival, documenting the creative protagonist's brilliant escape from the oppressive Midwest. Interesting story, but it's not mine.

My story goes like this: As a fresh-out-of-design-school grad, I was convinced by my very smart friend and mentor that I should build a better book of spec work and pass myself off as a competent junior copywriter. To do this, I read *One Show* books, drank pints and gallons of Guinness and Starbucks, and never went to sleep before 2 a.m., or before completing at least two spec ads.

This strict creative work regimen served me well, and with the support of my wife and guidance from my career sherpa, I pursued every single writing opportunity on every single known job site, board, or bank from coast to coast. I wrote thousands of introduction emails that led to hundreds of interviews and that won me a gaggle of gigs and only a handful of memorable full-time jobs (but many amusing, bizarre, and downright hysterical anecdotes I can now proudly draw from and share).

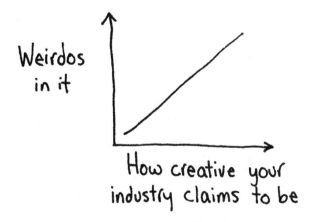

Professionally, I had my big-risk-big-city adventures in advertising, won a few awards, survived the great creative exodus of 2008, flirted with writing for famous fashion brands, and made some serious bank in pharmaland (yes, it was legal) before coming to rest in the education industry.

On the personal and passion project side, I returned to the heartland to start a family; I became a semi-legitimate music and travel journo; I created and abandoned blog after countless clever blog; and I was extremely fortunate enough to enjoy some borrowed time as a stay-at-home dad.

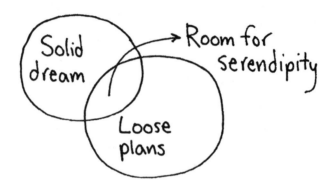

"Staying," in fact, has been my semi-pseudo sort-of-theme.

All of these little moments and big milestones, both personal and professional, wouldn't be possible without striving to stay. And because I operate better with lists, here is my guide to staying, in list form:

1. Stay Positive

Mindset is everything. I truly believe this. Craig Finn of The Hold Steady made it an anthem and helped me to remember this with his song and album of the same name, but family and friends are constant living reminders of this. As an eternal optimist, it is fairly easy for me to stay positive, but I can get down, get the blues, or get in a funk, too. It just takes a little extra mental nudge to coax the comeback. Compliments, exercise, coffee, and accomplishments (completion of small creative tasks and mundane duties alike) stave off bad vibes and excite the positive neurons.

2. Stay Busy

An occupied mind is a satisfied mind (mostly). I get a bigger rush from coming up with a host of new ideas and making small gains on my own manageable terms than arduously tilling over one new idea and stressing out over its flawless execution. For some, this translates to a lack of focus, but for me, it's about keeping myself interested and entertained so I can keep working on many things simultaneously. A blog post here, a magazine article there, and a few dozen more of each in my notebook, plus whatever "work" projects I'm currently working on.

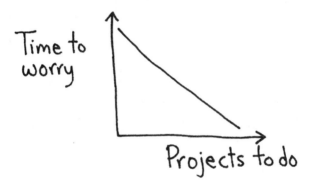

3. Stay Hungry

Blame it on John Lennon: I'm a dreamer. I'm constantly daydreaming and plotting and scheming to start the next version of Andy Warhol's Factory, form a Thermals cover band, or just trek across the country and write the book I'm always going on about. If it just sounds like talk to some or pipe dreams to others, who cares? These dreams drive me, keep me motivated, and help me create and complete countless other cool projects that pay or pave the way toward my greater goals.

4. Stay Connected

It is certainly cliché and automatic to tout staying connected as a key to success or whatever, but I'm talking less about networking and social presence and more about mindfully pursuing, growing, and maintaining both professional creative outlets and those linked to personal passion projects. Relevancy is itself irrelevant and subjective in the creative world, so all the weird, wacky, or completely square connections I have gathered over the years, I try to keep. There are ties I have to worlds that I don't visit as often, but I still contribute to, because there is still value there, be it benefits, perks, or other opportunities these worlds afford me.

5. Stay Put

The end goal of staying put is longevity. One year gives you experience, while one decade gives you expertise. In my early days, I was always trying to get "there." There, being the impossible utopian convergence of success and happiness through creative professional employment. The great irony is, I've gotten there (at least halfway) by staying put.

Through the years, staying put has taken on many meanings. Sometimes it was more literal, like staying in a position with a company longer than I might have wanted to, and sometimes it was more figurative, like sticking to my guns on a creative decision or betting on my hometown to be the perfect refuge for my kids to grow up in.

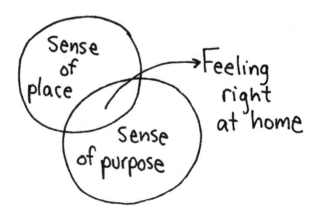

All in all, adapting to cubes and gray rooms with long tables and listening to people I'm supposed to respect use words like "methodology" incorrectly and say things like "we don't want to open Pandora's door" is a small stipend to pay for getting cushy corporate gigs that have allowed me to do what I love—and am decent enough at to have been able to do it for 10+ years.

And after all, while the pursuit of full-time creative work and the fulfillment that comes from obtaining it are short-lived, the realization that these passion projects and creative outlets are more important to my success and happiness than gainful creative employment is long-lasting.

Act on This

What do you want to stay with?

* * *

A person?

* * *

A place?

* * *

A thing?

* * *

A feeling?

* * *

A task?

* * *

A role?

* * *

Maybe nothing quite yet?

* * *

Look for your emotional anchors, and when you find them, drop them to define your material territory.

What Is an Artist's Place in the World?

JOSEPHINE DECKER,
FILM EDITOR
AND PERFORMANCE ARTIST

I find that airports make me feel both very, very big and very, very small. I have spent much of the past year in airports flying to film festivals. I am currently sitting in one on my way to Torino, Italy, where a retrospective on my work is being featured in a film festival. This feels preemptive. I am only thirty-three.

I started out in the news field, and somehow, news always feels important. News feels like—new! News is happening right now, and it's *so* important. People are dying.

My Zen teacher often says to me, "Do you use the day, or does the day use you?" Staring at the covers of the *New York Times*, I feel used by the day. I feel used by life. How have I been sitting in dark rooms contemplating my inner existence when there is so much world to live in?

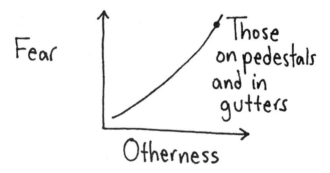

I am reminded of early artists, shamans who lived on the outskirts of their villages or camps so they could be more deeply connected to the world of the animals, the world of spirits.

We artists are invited to live there, too. Does it feel easy? Does it feel right? Does it feel perfect? It never feels like much of anything but confusing and hard. But that is what living with the spirits is. It's an invitation to the beyond.

Over the past three years, I have made two feature films. During this time, I would go long periods without any news of the outside world—sometimes on purpose.

I write at an artist residency called The School of Making Thinking, where I like to sit outdoors all day and meditate and then plunge in and not check the Internet at all. And then sometimes just out of necessity when I'm gunning for the Sundance deadline, I bury myself in the ground a bit. And only later hear that miners were trapped underground for six weeks and then rescued, that ISIS is a problem, and that pop musicians I've never heard of are much more famous than Britney Spears.

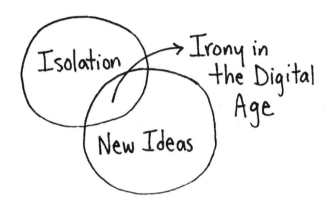

Disconnecting from culture may be foolish, may be backwards, may be a way of living in a narcissistic past. But these are the things I say to myself on a daily basis to admonish myself for not doing something relevant with my life—like writing for a TV show like *Community* or pounding the ground in Iraq to make brilliant, insightful CNN stories. These things feel exciting, culturally relevant, and inviting. You are part of a world of people who are passionately pursuing ideals and comedy and entertainment and information.

Meanwhile, I have been pursuing personal truth.

The Zen monks I train with are very clear, loving, gentle people. They live near Woodstock, NY, and read the *New Yorker* and sit in meditation anywhere between three and eleven hours a day, every day. They are living an isolated, maybe backwards, ancient lifestyle in a very modern world, and I am infinitely grateful they exist. They share with me something that I find literally nowhere else—a spiritual path. They inspire me to sit with my inner restlessness, my lack of peace; they inspire me to love myself despite my gluten fixations, my obsessive-compulsive work habits, and my failures at intimacy; and they ask me to challenge myself to be radically open.

This is also what artists do.

Sometimes, after a particularly clarifying session, I ask Ryushin, "Why go back out there? Why not just stay here forever?" And he says, "We train here. Here, we become clear, and when we are clear, we can go out into the world and be a mirror for what it is. We can go out into the world and reveal to the world what is happening, what we see, just by being clear."

When art is clear, it does this too. It reveals to an audience who the audience is. And what the world is that they live in. I don't mean: "You are a dynamic, sexually explosive person who lives on a farm." I mean: "My meaning is as deep as your meaning. My world is as deep as your world. Underneath Twitter is your desire. Underneath the mine is a pit in the center of the world. We are not so close to dying there. We are close to dying always."

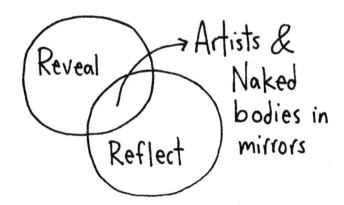

Do I feel as important as an artist? Sometimes. Do I feel like I am failing? Always. Do I feel like I *should* be doing something else with my life? Well, actually, no. I think I knew early on in life that I wanted to make my life a spiritual journey. I thought this would mean being a warrior—like picking up a stick or a big explosive stick or a huge explosive stick-like machine that could pursue the country's largest goals—but being a warrior has come to mean pursuing my goals. My personal small goals. It means being a warrior of my consciousness. It means guessing and hoping even when I would rather know absolutely that what I am doing is the right thing.

I don't know which war is harder.

Act on This

Appoint yourself the artist-in-residence of your own home—and do your work where you are. Declare a specific place to be your studio. Outline a series of works you will create, perform, or enjoy while in residence.

✳ ✳ ✳

When you begin to think of your work as art, you will give it more creative thought, more respectful attention, and it will move you further.

You Can Make Your Own Breaks

DONNA SALGADO,
DANCE ARTIST

The journey of a dancer is both discouraged and romanticized: Move to New York, make a living doing the ephemeral, get your name in lights. While the story is familiar, my journey as a dancer has been anything but cliché, yet I've learned there is something universal about the hustle.

The modern hustle requires one to define a personal spectrum of opportunities. In this spectrum, there are the big dreams, but there are also the tangential dreams, the practical fields, the areas of intrigue, the passion projects. Mapping my own spectrum has been a natural and recurring process of daydreaming and journaling. I exclude from the spectrum anything I don't feel like doing; if you wouldn't daydream about it, it isn't part of the big picture.

My daydreams have actually been the greatest compass for my career. I am a dancer through and through. I am built like a Rockette, I love the rush of performing, and I revel in the day-to-day maintenance and perfectionism of training. That said, I have always visualized choreography when listening to music. Long after a class is over, I have always contemplated the mechanics of the steps. These affinities have led me to work as a teacher and a choreographer; to direct my own dance company, Continuum Contemporary/Ballet; and most recently, to my creative involvement in a dance education brand for families—Crafterina. This whole portfolio of dance experiences has led me to my now preferred job title: Dance Artist.

For artistic thinkers and creatives, the modern hustle is more rigorous than ever before, mostly for three main reasons: the rise of amateurism (not necessarily a bad thing), the demands of social media (again, not necessarily bad), and the ability to get your work out there in a variety of avenues (a very good thing). This has created a bit of a shift in our culture, highlighting, ever so slightly, more indie artists who have normally been in the shadows of bigger organizations. In other words, there is more work out there, but you need to shine and, more importantly, you need to work to get noticed.

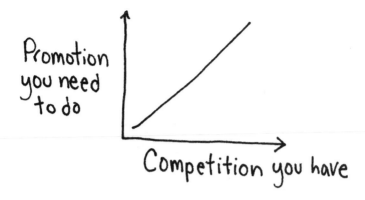

Promotion you need to do

Competition you have

For me, this has meant being really focused to support my multi-tasking. I need to attend classes on a daily basis to maintain my dance fluency. I also need to plant seeds daily for future projects, and I need to take on work for inspiration and pleasure. Doing these things offers positive rewards beyond the financial aspect. But because these necessities require time and energy, scheduling is key; there needs to be free time, wiggle room, and the ability for me to get eight hours of sleep.

My saving grace is working on a freelance, contractual basis. I create my own schedule, I know my own worth, and I demand the highest hourly wage possible for the work that I do. This is easier said than done, but it gets easier with seniority and with the multitude of cool things you do and add to your résumé.

Despite how rigorous I need to be in the pursuit of work, my passions are dance and choreography. I have had the opportunity to perform professionally in ballet and modern companies, perform in New York Fashion Week, choreograph a runway show, take my dance company on tour, choreograph for a Grammy award-winning pop star, accept university commissions, perform in art installations, and perform as a guest artist as the Sugar Plum Fairy in *The Nutcracker*. These are all experiences that I treasure. They are defining moments when I feel like I have lived the dream, and I feel blessed to have done so.

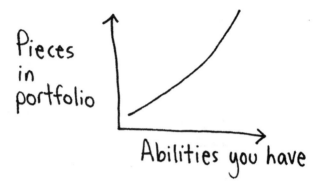

Along the way, I dabbled in writing for a dance magazine, instructing fitness classes, and modeling. I have a true New York story—I've tried everything and I've worked hard. My dedication to teaching has had a positive impact on my students and has given me the satisfaction of giving back, while being compensated fairly to do so. One of the great benefits of this hustle is that seemingly disparate skills I have learned in one area have actually informed me in other areas and have made me more marketable. Hustling actually makes you better.

Of course, there have been tough experiences along the way. I have not been paid for work I was supposed to be paid for on two occasions. I had to go to court. I have been in auditions where I felt I deserved the part and didn't get it. I have received my fair share of rejection letters and have been burned by some close colleagues.

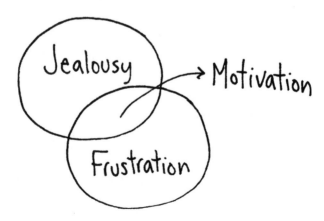

I've also learned that being good at hustling and having some success can give you some false friends and some jealous ones. And worse, at times, even the best of us can become momentarily jealous of the competition. These situations are unavoidable. They happen when you least expect it and can take you off course. But I think the best recourse is to be true to your dreams, your instincts, and your goals. Your hustle has nothing to do with anyone but yourself.

The best thing about the hustle is that you can define it. You dictate your dreams, your intrigues, and your passion projects, and you can pursue them. It requires a lot of time, so choose to defend your time with work that doesn't deplete you of your energy, while also paying you fairly.

Through the hustle you will get the chance to work on a variety of projects. You will get to work with many different people. You will put your ideas into the world. It will feel great.

My life has consisted of a lot of passion and a lot of hustle. Here are my top 15 tips for hustling:

1. Be proud of your hustle. If you are ashamed of any of the jobs you are doing, it will just drag you down.
2. Be proactive, not reactive. Focus on what it is that you want, not the competition.
3. Be friendly. Make friends. And support them when they begin doing their thing, too.
4. Accept your starting point. We all have to start somewhere.
5. Accept the seasons of your body and the game. Things change and you can ride the wave if you can accept the flow.
6. Spend wisely. Skip drinking. Skip that manicure. There: You've got lunch for a week!
7. Think big-picture. Think lessons. Think legacy. It will keep you inspired.
8. Follow through with your projects and ideas. Always.

9. Put your best-quality work out there.

10. Likewise, market and promote with your best-quality work and statements. (Spell-check!)

11. Credit your support system and don't neglect your personal life. (Thanks, Mom and Dad!)

12. Find your sources of inspiration and visit them when times get tough.

13. Always pay people on time when you owe them money. Get the money.

14. Tip well, make a donation, and support others. Good karma improves hustles.

15. Above all, stay true to you.

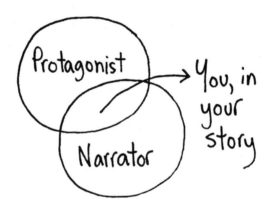

Act on This

Blurb yourself: Write ten compliments about your work,
as if they were written by someone else.

✳ ✳ ✳

Use these compliments as promotional
messages for yourself, and follow up each of those
statements with supporting examples
of your work.

✳ ✳ ✳

You'll get a little boost of confidence and give
yourself talking points for new business conversations.

Once Bitten, Never Cured

ALEX PEARLMAN,
RECOVERING ENTREPRENEUR
AND DIGITAL NEWS GIRL

There are two ways to get bitten by the entrepreneur bug.

The first is genetic. People with this gene, you know who you are. You can't help wanting to tinker, going your own way, or regularly showing authority figures impolite hand gestures—and you answer to no one. This is like being born double-jointed—it can't be helped. And sure, with time, maybe the inclination to run away from a preordained life track will fade, but even if you try to cover it up, the urge to be an entrepreneur will continue to re-emerge. Some people are just born this way.

The second way is circumstance. Chance, luck, serendipity, whatever you want to call it. For a lot of people in my generation specifically (*millennials* is the accepted term), the circumstances surrounding our entrée into the "real world" were dismal. Many of us were forced to give up big dreams of desk jobs and security and figure something else out.

I had a degree in print journalism, a minor in philosophy, and an internship that had almost no hope of turning into a secure stream of income. I didn't want to do what most journalism students were doing, which was either writing briefs and answering phones at dying print organizations or going to work at a PR agency for "the man." So I joined a fledgling journo/marketing project, with the mission to turn a less-than-mediocre blog into a crowdsourced online magazine.

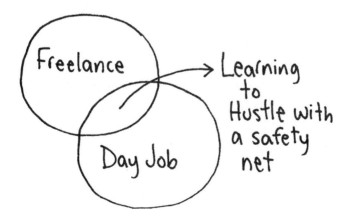

After two and a half years and a lot of freelancing on the side, I parlayed being the cofounder and editor of the online magazine into a real job at one of those aforementioned print newspapers. I started another website for "the youths," as well as managed a number of other projects. But I was pleasantly surprised to find that the working style I had adopted while freelancing and managing a shoestring startup in the real world worked just as well when I put it to use managing a shoestring startup within a newspaper. I'm told that this lifestyle is called "hustling."

But the hustle can also have a serious downside: extreme mood swings and worrying levels of depression. According to a recent series of polls by Gallup, entrepreneurs and freelancers are more stressed and worried than any other American workers. They are also more likely to feel optimism and are more interested in their work. A range of industry publications, from the *Guardian*'s tech section to *Inc.* magazine, have begun to talk about how this lifestyle can have dramatic impact on overall mental health, and it's great that it is finally becoming less of a taboo to talk about.

Without wanting to diminish the very real struggle faced by diagnosed bipolar individuals, I can't think of anything else to compare the stress of day-to-day life as an entrepreneur or freelancer.

The slightest good news can shoot me into a soaring seizure of maniacal self-congratulatory glee that can last for days. When I do something well and my ideas move forward, I feel like I'm on a roll and I can do no wrong. I think positive thoughts: *I will be successful! I will be happy! I will be able to show my face at my high school reunion!*

These are the days my body produces the steam that powers my brain wheels, that makes it physically possible to push myself through large veggie pizzas, multiple bottles of red wine, and the sleepless, active nights when I do my best work. This energy is what propelled me to every single startup networking event and party

Boston had to offer for four years, and the race to cover every base and shake every hand.

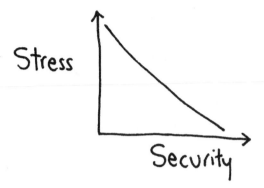

But the slightest bad luck or dropped ball, and I am driven into a state of suicidal melancholy punctuated by bouts of Netflix bingeing, ignoring emails from work and my mother, and a bad habit of convincing myself that either everyone I know secretly hates me, or they believe it's only a matter of time until I fuck up.

When the stock invested in my projects is the blood, sweat, and tears of a very small team, the burden is enormous. I don't have the safety of a corporation at my back, or the luxury to work an eight-hour day. (Who are those people?) The startup lifestyle can be mentally debilitating, especially because I know something my friends, investors, and employees don't: Those success projections aren't based on science; rather, they're based on my abilities—and most days I don't believe I possess the qualities necessary to get the job done. And I'll have no one to blame but myself when I fail.

I have heard for years from mentors and mentees alike that I am "fearless," that I "push boundaries," that I'm a "radical," that I am "admired." Let's just be clear about the fact that to me, this is all bullshit. Professors have asked me to mentor younger students, managers have forced interns under my wing, and a lot of times I don't know why.

Mostly this just causes me more stress. Not believing in yourself and your abilities, I'm told, is another sign of depression.

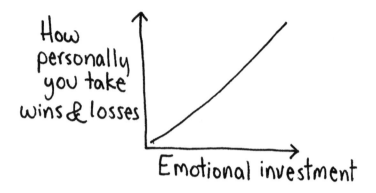

This rapid fluctuation between the highs and the lows is a trait often found in intensely creative and ambitious people. We put all of our eggs into baskets made of our own ideas and plug the holes with dumb luck.

We are pot-smoking paranoiacs with a whole host of à la carte social and performance anxieties, and we don't know how to deal. We are students of the school of Fake It Till You Make It, and I am the valedictorian. Knowing this, however, doesn't make it any easier.

So, how do I deal? Sometimes I don't, and I give up for days.

But mostly, when I get stressed and messed and start to unravel, I try to take a deep breath and think about something that isn't work-related that's going well, or something that is positive.

I'll admit that, for a long time, the only thing I could think of was that my cat really loved me. About 75 percent of the reason I never killed myself when I lived alone and ran that magazine was because I didn't trust my beloved cat, Prudence, not to eat my face off before someone found me. Because let's be honest, a cat is a cat, and as much as she nuzzles my nose, nature would compel her to chow down on my lifeless body. Which would make us both sad, and totally grossed out. So I didn't commit suicide.

But then, after years of internal struggle, something bizarre happened.

More good things that weren't work-related started to hog center stage in my life. It took a very long time and a lot of introspection, but I finally feel like taking a year off from the treadmill of career climbing to do some art, and it won't be the worst thing ever. FOMO (fear of missing out) is no longer a thing that controls my life, and I'm pretty sure digital journalism will still be there when I'm done fucking around with some interesting new ideas.

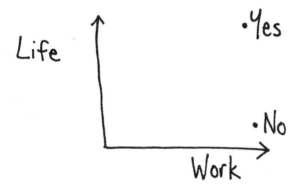

Life is calling. That cat needs to be nuzzled, the dogs need to be walked, and my partner needs my love and attention. So if the project has to wait a day, I finally understand that that's OK.

But it's always rosy from the other side of the tunnel, right? And just as I'm starting to figure out how to live with the day-to-day melee of my chosen lifestyle, there's always someone else who is still stuck in the muck.

My mother recently quit her job and started her own company doing consulting for commercial building owners who are looking to make eco-friendly renovations. Now she's hustling, too, and she's exhausted. (Remember what I said about genetics and the bug? I don't make this shit up.)

Some days she calls me and in one breath is all like, "Wooooo! I got three more contracts! And I went to this networking event, and it was packed with all these really smart people! And then the organizer said he knew who I was! HE KNEW WHO I WAS! And he introduced me to, like, twenty other really big people! And then I finished this really great presentation and took it to the board of this other building and they loved it, and I wasn't even nervous and I answered all their questions and it was great! WOOOO!"

But then the other day she called, and it was a rainy day in London. I was walking to the bus stop, and there was something in her voice that made me wait two buses to get off the phone with her.

"[Sigh.] Hi. . . How's it going?" She sounded like Eeyore.

"It's OK! I'm walking to the bus and I'm going shopping. What's up with you, Mom?"

"[Sigh.] Well, I just have too much to do. And then that guy I hired who is so good said at the staff meeting that he's quitting. And the intern kid just does not know how to do a spreadsheet, and this whole project got messed up, and now it's going to be late. And I got another contract, but I thought the guy I hired was going to be with me to help, and now it's just so much for one person, and I just feel very sad, like I won't finish everything in time, or I won't do it well, and I feel terrible."

I knew that all I could do was be there and listen, and make sure she knew that I didn't think she was going to fail. And even if she did, living means more than success with a startup project. She sounded like a broken record when she was saying this stuff to me all those years, but it ended up being true, and I repeated it back to her.

It was clear to me that my mother caught the entrepreneur bug too, and I realized that her emotional seesaw wasn't just *our* problem—it's a universal one. It's a side effect of the virus you catch from spending too much energy on your money-making idea. And like any impossible virus, there is no cure for this bug, only acceptance of it.

Mental health professionals say it's responsible to care for clinical depression by preparing for its onset, like shutting the storm windows on a house. The life of the hustler isn't different. But by knowing what to expect, it's possible to forecast the looming negative effects of the entrepreneur bug on your mind and body.

They're not going anywhere, and there is no way to fix them, but there is wisdom in acceptance of our flaws. Once I understood that the mood swings and the depression and the frenzied glee are a certain and indisputable part of my future, it became that much easier to deal with it, set it aside, and keep plugging on with the next great idea.

Act on This

List your fears about your work—the terrible things that make you wince and cringe.

* * *

You may have never said them out loud, or even thought about them for longer than a stinging moment, so this might be difficult.

* * *

Once you've articulated those fears, write down the opposite of your fears—those are your goals.

* * *

Acknowledging both ends of the success spectrum will help you cope with ups, downs, and sideways situations.

Respect the Catalysts

DANTE SHEPHERD,
PROFESSOR AND WEB COMIC

I got insanely lucky once I decided I wanted to be a professor. And that was a necessary catalyst on top of my existing long-term plan that I was executing to the letter.

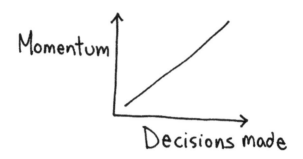

Most likely, your view of the Hustle Economy involves something flexible, adept-to-adapt. With consumer interest rapidly fluctuating, rapidly peaking, and rapidly sinking, heroes of the Hustle Economy are prepared for anything and everything. This certainly is true.

But this perspective misses the fact that in order to have achieved that status as someone who can be flexible and survive, you had to develop and grow and keep overcoming a somewhat delineated series of barriers before you could be at an Optimal Stage of succeeding and hustling. If you step back far enough, you can see you were jumping past barrier after barrier dating all the way back to your very beginning.

There's a series of stages that you have to pass through in our increasingly structured and regimented world, where some minimal expectation of learning is required before you're allowed to move to the next stage.

First, you get about five years in Baby Stage, when you only have to learn how to become self-aware and how to form memories.

Then, six years in Adolescent Stage, when you only have to learn some basic skills and relatively rudimentary knowledge.

Then, seven years in Preparatory Stage, when you only have to learn what field you want to learn more about.

Then, four years in Specialist Stage, when you only have to learn what aspect of the field you want to achieve.

Then, X years in Second Preparatory Stage, when you only have to learn how to jump through the series of hoops required to get to the goal you may have decided upon in the Specialist Stage.

Then, X years in Optimal Stage, when you've finally reached the position you started working toward seventeen + X years ago.

Finally, X years in Retirement Stage, when you only have to learn what the hell else you can do with your life.

And then you die.

Meanwhile, there's a leap in between each stage. In science, we would refer to this barrier as activation energy—the concept in chemistry that, when two reactants have the potential to react, there's a minimum amount of energy that needs to be put into the system in order for the reaction to be achieved. Without that much energy, you get no reaction. Plotted out in terms of energy versus reaction path, activation energy is literally represented as the hump you need to get over to get to the final products.

It's an obvious metaphor (or obvious, at least, if you're obsessed with chemistry) to real-life situations. There's the potential in every system, every group, every person for a grand achievement to be seized, to be realized, but you need to get over that hump for that potential to be synthesized, to be reacted upon, to be produced. Sometimes this activation energy is minimal, to the extent that simply aging will boost you to the next Stage; other times, the barrier is utterly daunting.

Chemically speaking, we can reduce this activation energy by introducing a catalyst into the system. The catalyst acts to modify the transition state between reactants and product, providing a middle ground with a simpler hump to get over, with less energy needed for potential to become outcome. So, while we still have a barrier to progress at each Stage, through catalysis we can get a boost in order to achieve our desired potential.

In order to succeed and out-hustle the Hustle Economy, you're reliant on two major factors: a plan and luck. You may not have clearly planned it all out from the beginning, but you certainly kept developing plans or pieces of plans along the way to get there. And even then, you're going to need some beneficial catalysts.

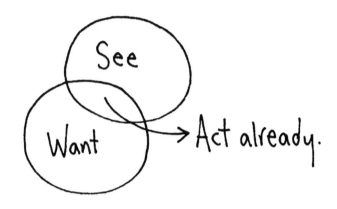

Back to my attempt to become a professor: When I made the decision, realizing what my Optimal Stage would be, I'd certainly put in time, effort, and energy to that point, and would certainly put in more time, energy, and effort while continuing on before achieving my dream position. But when I was twenty and decided I wanted to be a professor, I only had X + two more years ahead of me before I could reach my Optimal Stage. And I had a relatively firm idea of what that X would look like:

After two more years to graduate college, I'd then need to spend five or six or seven or eight years in graduate school getting a doctorate (all depending on how successful I was with the research), meaning I'd have the acceptable paper document to be allowed potential eventual access to professorship. Then I'd spend two or three or four or five years working as post-doctoral researcher, meaning I'd have the expected service in an intermediate role that would allow the professorial gatekeepers to deem me potentially acceptable.

And then I'd have to actually get the job.

But I was incredibly fortunate to have made that realization of what my Optimal Stage looked like at the relatively young age of twenty. Certainly there are incredibly deep and interesting and wonderful people who don't realize until much later what their Optimal Stage might actually be, and they spend years in a tangential Wandering Stage exploring and experiencing, only to have some unknown X once they began to settle into a final goal. If they're lucky, their Wandering will have doubled as their dose of Preparatory, but too often they end up needing to double back to some previous stage and try working forward again.

Catalysts kept boosting me forward from that point, fortunately. My second day in a laboratory in graduate school, I obtained scientific results that were better than everything my laboratory predecessor had spent his five years reporting. Instead of having to spend an undetermined length of time working toward grand results, I just needed to fill in the time figuring out how I had done what I had done. A jump up to the right next level, just because I happened to pour the right mixture of chemicals onto a 1cm x 1cm slab.

Catalysts kept boosting me. I went to a conference during my second year of graduate school and ended up spending several nights drinking with a seemingly random conference attendee who had intense eyes that held a kind of crazy eye gleam about them—the kind of guy who could hold court when telling a story. He started regaling me with these unbelievable yarns, telling me how he blew up a bridge when he was seven years old, how when he was in college, some guys went into his room to haze him while he was asleep and he put two of them in the hospital WHILE HE WAS STILL ASLEEP. There was even stories about all the research he did with fire (because of course a guy like that did research with fire).

Every night that followed, for the rest of the conference, I drank with him and got him to retell those stories. Three years later when I needed a postdoctoral position, I happened to run into him at another conference. I remembered his crazy eyes, not his credentials, but when I reintroduced myself, I learned he was a major scientist at a government research institute. He quickly set me up with the right connections and helped guide me into a research fellowship at a top-notch government laboratory. A jump up to the right next Stage, just because I drank with a guy and didn't run away when he let his eyes get wild and crazy. That's a catalyst.

Catalysts kept boosting me. When nearing the end of my postdoctoral position, I was in the muck and mire of applying for professorships and getting rejected left and right (and getting rejected by many more without ever being told I was rejected). My applications certainly had strong teaching credentials, but were likely being pulled down by the lack of cumulative research achievements. Then, I came across a position with a confusing title, and while several people didn't think it was worth my time (including my boss), I was at that moment suffering from stress-related sleep deprivation.

To illustrate, I was so sleep deprived I began talking to the chair I would collapse into each night. Even worse, I was pretty sure the chair was responding to me. At which point, because it seemed like a good idea to me (who was actively hallucinating), I asked the chair what I should do. I believe it responded, "I cannot talk to you. I am a chair. You should probably seek medical attention. Again, I am a chair. But you may as well submit your application."

So, I submitted the Hail Mary application. Literally the next day I was asked to set up a phone interview, and two days later I got a call from the acting chair of the department, who just happened to work at the same research institution I was currently working at, and I just happened to know the same people he had been affiliated with. I got invited to the only interview opportunity I would receive and was offered the position. A jump up to the right Optimal level, just because I happened to throw a Hail Mary when the person reviewing the applications had the right connections.

As if that weren't enough, my luck seemed magnified in other ways, looking back.

I decided I wanted to be a teaching professor, a relatively rare position in an academic industry driven by laboratory research. Achieving relatively significant success in my minimal research achievements certainly boosted my potential and helped disguise the areas in which I was dramatically lacking.

I made the mistake of telling my advisor that I didn't really care about research when I was two years into graduate school. The graduate advisor basically has you in his indentured servitude as he sees fit for as long as he sees fit. Getting propelled forward by him anyway was utterly fortunate, just on the face of it.

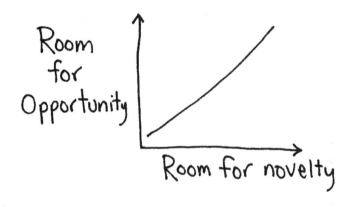

Just wanting to be a professor and then actually getting to be one requires a tremendous amount of luck. There are potential candidates who file applications to over eighty colleges during the annual announcements of open positions, figuring that any professor position is better than none at all. I ended up applying to sixteen colleges and had to deal with institutions that either completely lacked my passion for teaching ("Well, you clearly know how to demonstrate enthusiasm for research, so clearly you'll be a great teacher") or lacked social graces (one rejection letter left incomplete but mailed anyway literally read

"Thank you for your recent application for the position of {custom-text100121}") or lacked any real interest in me at all. Chancing into a position when far-more-qualified candidates are left to return to their postdoctoral work for another few years feels like finding a rabbit's foot sprouting a four-leaf clover.

So what is the lesson in all this? To succeed in the Hustle Economy, the truth is that you need both luck and to execute a plan. You need to know what your Optimal Stage is. You need to know what you have to do to get there. Yes, luck will be able to push you over those activation energy barriers and provide boosts, but you need to do the work to put yourself in those positions to be able to benefit from that luck.

You have to meet the ever-growing list of prerequisites in terms of knowledge and previous experience and references in order to be eligible. That means determination to accumulate the expected minimal knowledge and expertise, then going beyond that and accumulating more knowledge and more experience in order to be desirable. This means maintaining and using all those years of school to keep building upon your level of knowledge and level of understanding, specializing and further specializing as appropriate while maintaining a degree of breadth.

You have to be willing to run the gauntlet, to know that there are years of work and effort and intermediacy. There are obstacles to pass, flaming hoops to jump through, needles to thread, and fingers to cross. Meanwhile, you'll feel frustration, depression, loss of purpose, loss of motivation, fear of failure, boredom, physical inertia, mental inertia, and a gamut of other emotions that will readily mix and combust at any moment's notice, potentially forcing you back to the start and having to begin your launch all over again.

You have to enter the labyrinth of emotions and education, probably feeling lost and getting lost on more than one occasion, even if you're given the map to guide you out to your Optimal Stage.

If a catalyst happens to cross your path when you're more interested in lying aimlessly around and slacking off, you might be granted the good fortune of discovering one more leftover frozen burrito at the back of the freezer instead of the good fortune of being offered your dream job. Not that the frozen burrito won't be delicious and rewarding in itself, but it may not be worth the grand trade you've inadvertently made.

And truthfully, there's a third element necessary beyond luck and planning. You need an outlet.

You have to discover other passions you can use to counteract the emotional distress of being so far from experiencing your Optimal passion. I ended up taking pictures of myself standing in front of a blackboard while dressed in a baseball cap and a lab coat, writing jokes and fake wisdom on the board and posing next to the words in chalk, then posting the photocomics on the Internet. It was all a means to produce a creative outlet to distract myself from how long I had to wait to be a professor, yet it somehow gained an audience. It became a way to interact with people and prevent professional depression from setting in.

This is largely how I'm recognized. On my first day as a professor, the first class of students recognized me from my creative passion, which helped me cement a stronger bond with them and helped me become a better teacher and a better professor.

Luck, again. But you've got to strive and work before luck will strive and work for you.

I think about this all the time. If you think of activation energy, the barriers that I had to overcome to land in this perfect position were not only one after another, but they had dramatically high peaks to overcome. If a couple of perfect, miraculous catalysts hadn't landed in my lap, I would never have been able to achieve what was necessary, despite all the personal energy and work I put in to try to produce something from my potential. This leads to the obvious question: If it's always luck serving to catalyze personal success, what is the point of putting in the effort? Which is, of course, misleading and ignores the many Stages you overcame and the plan you put in place and the outlet you relied on.

So, here's what I've come to believe after years of contemplation on the matter. Yes, you can set up the right reaction. You and your credentials and your interests and your potential may be the right ingredients, and maybe you will be able to overcome that activation energy and produce something great based entirely off the energy from your own hard work. But every so often there will be a catalyst thrown your way, some stroke of luck, and it may lead you to your dream job, based on how hard you were working at getting there, or it may just lead you to find an extra frozen burrito in the freezer because you are hungry. These catalytic moments come, and appear lucky, bizarre, and completely non-scientific, but they really do appear for you to take full advantage of. You just have to be ready and focused so you can make something of that potential, and so that your hard work will be enough.

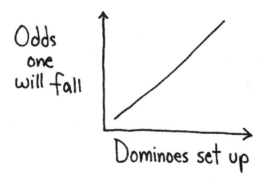

You want to succeed in this Hustle Economy? Plan. Find an outlet. Be ready for luck. Maybe you'll find yourself reacting to your potential, activation barriers far behind you.

Act on This

Give social serendipity room to happen.

* * *

Do this by putting yourself (physically or digitally)
into a situation (at least once a week, forever) where you
can meet, help, or observe someone who does the
type of work that you want to do.

How to Crowdfund Anything
(AKA How to Launch a Product)

BRAD O'FARRELL,
GAME MAKER

In 2013, I crowdfunded a card game called Story War on Kickstarter. It was an unknown brand that raised $360,000 from over 7,000 people. I had never done a Kickstarter project before, and I had to figure everything out as I went. I want to teach you how to crowdfund something, assuming crowdfunding still exists by the time you read this. But if crowdfunding dies, something else will rise up and replace it, and this advice should still hold.

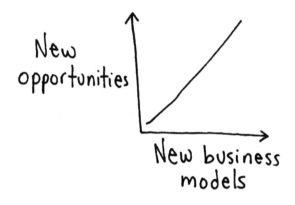

The principles described in this essay are used to talk about crowdfunding, but they could just as easily be applied to a basket weaving business in 1836, or a laser drug factory in 2525. Because these tips aren't really about a platform—they're about human nature. And platforms like Kickstarter exist as a mirror of human nature. The tools at your disposal might change, but the wiring of human brains will not.

Come up with a good product.

The first and most important step to crowdfunding something is to come up with something that would do well on a crowdfunding platform. This is where a lot of projects die before they even get started.

You might think crowdfunding would be a good way to make that game or book or movie idea you've been kicking around in your head since high school. But you're probably wrong. Because that idea that has been incubating in your head for years is probably already too dated, too personal, and reverse engineered around your own preferences. It probably won't work well on a crowdfunding platform.

Instead of thinking, "I want to crowdfund my secret brain thing," you should be thinking, "What is a new thing I could come up with that would do well as a crowdfunded project?" First, look at all the projects that are already successful. What is it that they all have in common?

No, I'm not talking about zombies, steampunk, and Cthulhu, although that's part of it. You'll find that most successful crowdfunding projects center around a core novel idea that makes people say, "Oh, wow, that's cool." You need to come up with an idea that makes people say that. You need to come up with a bunch of ideas and tell your friends about them, and see which ones they think are cool. If enough friends tell you one of your ideas is cool, it probably is. If you get a lukewarm response, you should move on and try something else.

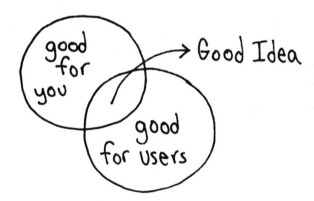

Once you have an idea that gets a positive response from your friends, you should test it out on people you don't know very well. Talk about it at parties to friends-of-friends, or PM it to someone you barely know on Facebook. Try to encourage harsh feedback. If your idea survives and consistently excites people, it's probably a good one. Now you just need to figure out how to communicate that idea to a stranger as quickly as possible.

You're not given much time to make an impression on the Internet, and the quicker you can communicate an idea and get people to the "oh cool" realization, the better. Zombie projects are popular because it's an aesthetic shorthand that means "few vs. many combat." Steampunk is shorthand for "gadgets and puzzles and fashion." These aesthetic shorthands are popular because they are public domain brands that can efficiently communicate the familiar part of an idea to the audience, making the unfamiliar part understandable much faster.

You'll need to be a little bit more populist and a little bit more pandering than you'd probably like to be, but hey, this is crowdfunding. You need to play to the crowd.

You only launch once.

I have no opinion on Steve Jobs as a man, but as shoulder angels go, he's the worst. So many young entrepreneurs have bought into the Jobs mythos that a self-assured "F you" attitude is the secret to success. Part of the reason the WWSJD philosophy is so popular is because it's so self-serving.

Who wouldn't want to believe that their first instincts are right and that the world is full of idiot sheeple who can't wrap their head around you, the misunderstood visionary? This idea is toxic and almost always leads to failure. And it's probably also not the way Steve Jobs actually ran his business.

You should realize that your first instincts are probably going to be wrong. The Dunning–Kruger effect describes a cognitive bias where inexperienced individuals overestimate their own competency and underestimate the skills of others.

If you launch your product using your own initial expectations, you will probably fail. Then you'll wish you could go back in time and do the whole thing over again with all the new things you learned. And you'll probably write a blog post about it.

But there's another way! Instead of rushing in like an idiot, you can drink the tears of other idiots and absorb their powers.

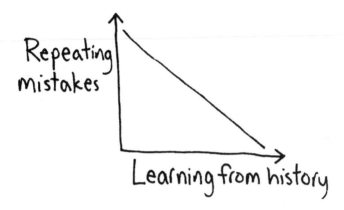

Seek out "crowdfunding postmortem" blog posts and read them. Read as many as you can find. Read the success stories and the failures. Look at what they have in common and what was done differently. You'll find that a lot of people came to similar conclusions. And you can use these conclusions to plan your campaign before you launch it.

Should you do a $1 reward tier? No, the credit card transaction fees will eat your revenue and steal sales from your next tier up. Should you sell T-shirts? Maybe, but calculate the profit margins first and find a T-shirt fulfillment company to handle that for you. Should you sell posters? Heck no, they are awkward and expensive to ship because of the weird cardboard tube thing. All these questions and more can be easily answered by the simple act of researching before you do something.

Marketing is easy if you never sleep.

Finally, after months of research and planning, it's time to launch your campaign. Get ready for all of your research to suddenly become useless.

You'll find that research can only take you so far. There are too many unique quirks to your campaign and too many unknown variables to account for. You won't really know how to promote your campaign until you're actually looking at the stats on a day-to-day basis and freaking out about it.

But don't worry! You've got a sophisticated secret weapon at your disposal: trial and error. Try every kind of marketing tactic you can think of. Spamming your former co-workers. Maybe try posting it on your mom's Facebook wall. Is Reddit still a thing? Do ANYTHING you think might work, monitor whether or not it does work, and repeat the things that do work.

When I ran my campaign, I thought the biggest source of traffic would be viral Tumblr posts. But we exhausted that audience pretty quickly. It turns out my game got the most new backers when it cross-promoted with other games on Kickstarter. I asked other people running projects at the same time if they wanted to give each other mutual shoutouts in backer updates. This had a huge impact on sales; it turns out it's way easier to get someone to back a project if they've backed something else before. As soon as I figured that out, I switched gears and made cross-promotion the focus of my campaign.

This is not to say that cross-promotion will work for you every time. I'm saying that you should try a bunch of stuff and repeat what works and stop doing what doesn't. This is easily the most arduous part of running a crowdfunding campaign and not something you can really pawn off to a PR agency. No one is going to fight for you as hard as you can fight for yourself, not for any amount of money.

Do you want fries with that?

About halfway through your campaign, you should be feeling pretty good. You've got a few real customers now! They like your product! They like you! They're going nuts for your thing! It's time to milk them for all they're worth.

It's way easier to up-sell existing customers than find new ones. That's the short answer for why capitalism made Americans fat. If people are so excited about your thing that doesn't even exist yet that they're willing to give you $20, they might be excited enough to give you $40. Try it.

You'll want reasonable reward tiers with a price that you choose based on research. It might be $10, $20, or $30; it depends on the value of your product. But pretty soon, you'll see that one of your tiers is clearly the most popular. That's your cue to make the tier immediately above it way cooler and constantly talk about how much cooler the more expensive tier is in backer updates. By incentivizing your backers to switch to a more expensive tier, you could potentially double your revenue without gaining a single new customer.

Always remember that your existing customers are your most valuable resource. You can get so much more out of them than money. You can get some great feedback on your actual product. You can ask them to promote your project on their social media feeds. Heck, you can even use them as a bargaining chip to initiate cross-promotions with other campaigns (e.g., "Plug my thing to your people, and I'll plug your thing to my people!").

Just don't forget that this is more about them than it is about you. If a lot of people start angrily pushing back against your wacky schemes to grow your campaign, it might be time to cool your jets and try another tactic. The difference between a crowd and a mob is subtle, so be careful.

If you knew what you were doing, you wouldn't be here.

Congratulations, your campaign has been dramatically overfunded, and you suddenly realize you have no idea what you're doing! How does mass producing things in China work? Can I just mail stuff with regular stamps? How do I get a barcode? Are taxes a thing? You're going to have to spend the next year or so figuring all this stuff out!

But don't worry, it's cool: People will be banging on your door begging to help you out. Most of the problems you'll have can be solved by a company or consultant that specializes in solving that very specific problem. Their potential client base is so small that they'll be coming to you! And then you'll have to learn to tell the difference between a good sales pitch and a bad sales pitch.

A good strategy for finding out if a fulfillment agency is legit is to go behind their backs and talk to their biggest clients. The agency will probably list all their big clients on their website, along with a carefully curated quote. You can use that to find the client's contact info and reach out to them. Usually when people regret a business arrangement, they won't say anything publicly, but they'll probably drop hints in an off-the-record, one-on-one conversation.

If a fulfillment agency looks shady, Google whatever service they're claiming to provide and find their competitors. Talk around and pit them against each other until you get the best offer. Don't be timid about it—this stuff is important!

Once you've taken other people's money, it's too late to say you're "bad at the business stuff." If this whole thing falls apart, you could face a ruined reputation, legal action, or worse! I know at least two people who ended up in actual psychiatric hospitals because of the overwhelming stress of a mismanaged crowdfunding campaign. No pressure.

Also remember that a product isn't necessarily a business. Finding a small community of early adopters is the easy part; the hard part is generating consistent sales to the general public. This is a classic business problem, and you can learn more about it by reading the book *Crossing the Chasm* by Geoffrey A. Moore, which was published in 1991, but is still very relevant to startups today. You'll need to start thinking about how to turn your product into a sustainable business as soon as your campaign ends.

Obviously you'll want your business to succeed, but what if it doesn't? You're going to have to make a contingency plan for all levels of success, including total failure. Make sure you always leave enough money in the bank account for your exit strategy; you don't want to one day realize you spent everything on fulfilling the project and have no money left to pay your rent.

You're probably going to feel like your creation is the most important thing in your life (your Heisenberg meth) and that nothing else matters. And while it's very productive to feel that way, remember to be a human being. Remember that you'll eventually need to go back to sleeping and showering on a regular schedule even if you don't have a day job.

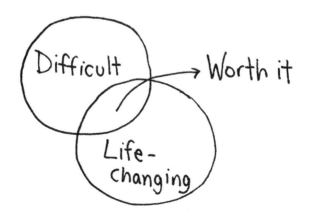

Remember that all your dreams coming true doesn't mean your life stops happening. When this is all over—and one day, it will all be over—you're going to feel like a totally different person. But it'll be worth it.

Now go forth and hustle.

Act on This

Get a few decades of secondhand experience.

* * *

Build a case-study library and let other people's experience guide your next steps.

* * *

Bookmark, download, or otherwise find at least fifty stories of either success or failure in your realm of business.

* * *

Scan for key themes, repeated behaviors, and red flags. Remember these stories as you work on your next big thing.

How to Customize Your Career

JESS KIMBALL LESLIE, TRENDSPOTTER

I am a freelance trendspotter. Yes, that's a thing. Yes, I can prove it. Yes, I make a full, honest, fulfilling living this way, and doing so takes a tremendous amount of hustle.

I write about nascent trends in media, technology, and culture that I suspect will go mainstream; I've had reports commissioned by everyone from fashion icons to news agencies to governments to advertising firms.

I got into trendspotting because I've been unduly obsessed with the future since childhood. As a 1990s preteen, I managed both a Prodigy and an America Online account along with four dozen strangers-slash-pen pals. People on these *Flintstones*-era social networks saw the future early; we knew that sending messages across screens was hugely innovative, and that the technology would change the world. Since then, I've always wanted to know about what the next thing is, and preferably, to know about it first.

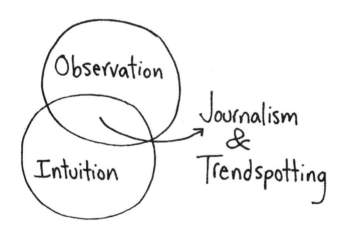

The trendspotting process is similar to a journalist's process; I constantly interview the world's academics, inventors, authors, and entrepreneurs about their latest projects. With enough good input, it's possible to see patterns in how disparate creative people are thinking, to see the cool companies when they're small, and the great performers when nobody above 14th Street cares.

I learned how to write trendspotting reports while working regular 9-to-5 jobs (believe it or not, there are a multitude of companies that professionally "spot trends"), but eventually I was able to write a great trendspotting report by myself. The truth of the new economy is that if you have a skill, you don't need a job; if you can produce something by yourself that people need, then you can sell it by yourself, too.

So you have a skill—how do you then parlay it into successful freelancing? The secret is not in learning how to "be your own brand" or "networking" or "tweeting"; I hate all of those things. The secret to freelancing is in learning how to be a great meeting. What do I mean?

Every single day, millions of adult professionals arrive at work only to be bored shitless by meetings that, by my account, should legally be considered war crimes. Most meetings are an ice cream sundae of PowerPoints, sales charts, target audiences, insights, windbags, and relevance, topped off with a whipped cream poison of "team-building" exercises. These meetings accomplish only one thing—destroying man's will to live. If, by comparison, *you* can become one of the day's good meetings, that's meaningful. Just be reasonably cool, funny, and fun to hang out with on projects. Seriously.

If you can also solve a problem and not get flustered when someone else takes all the credit, then congratulations, people will hire and rehire you as a freelancer. As my very successful self-employed friend Jumana taught me long ago, "freelancer" is just another way to say that you're a client's secret weapon. Learn to operate humbly and accordingly.

There are, of course, other life skills you will need. Freelancing for many years means that you have to learn how not to spend money, even when you're lucky enough to have some. When you have a million dollars, when you can live for the rest of your life without ever working again, then you have my permission to spend some of your money. Until then, it's imperative to remember that you are outside the system. Get a stupid *Fight Club* poster from your college friend, I don't care, just realize that people with 9-to-5 jobs are protected in ways that you are not; they have far better job stability, benefits, company-sponsored retirement savings plans, paid travel expenses, even pensions. I laughed at these things—until the day I didn't have them.

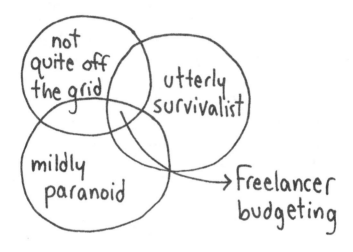

When I am not freelancing, I'm writing personal essays about my experience with technology for popular and unpopular literary magazines. Despite having received a moderate amount of attention, publishing is an industry that so far has paid me exactly one lobster. Freelancing as a trendspotter for many months of the year gave me the time and opportunity to treat writing as a hobby at first, which was financially (and emotionally) very helpful in the ten years it took me to get published. If you, too, have your eye on one of the impossible high-prestige, typically low-pay careers (writing, acting, music-making, pictures), then I highly suggest becoming smart at one of the high-paying freelance careers, too, such as graphic design and coding.

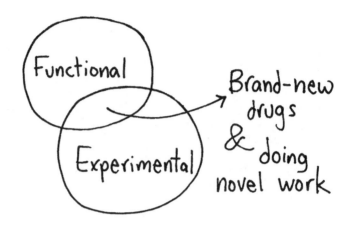

Freelancing, at its best, is the ability to support yourself while trying out slightly different versions of your career, your life, yourself. It's the ability to keep evolving, to not confine yourself to a corporate job's expectations of what your life should become. Understand what freelancing is and isn't, and you'll be in the best position to take advantage of what it is.

Act on This

Embrace your role as a sidekick.

* * *

Think of all the ways you can make someone
else look good, seem smarter, get more done, or otherwise
be an excellent and beneficial asset.

* * *

Now, line those functions up with your expertise,
and articulate the specific assistance you can offer.

* * *

Congrats: You've just positioned yourself
as the ideal freelancer.

Why Everyone Needs a Business Partner

MEREDITH HAGGERTY,
PUBLISHING ENTREPRENEUR

I've never really been a business human, so I never expected to have a business partner. I have rarely made money and mostly made jokes, and Jokes About Business has been one of my very favorite categories for years.

In college I majored in English but enjoyed visiting my friends at Stern School of Business, barking orders into an imaginary cell phone, "Buy! Sell! Tell China to offload our assets! I'm getting a fax! Beep bop boop beep." After school, I stayed out of business, working first as an editorial assistant at a literary agency—where I willfully refused to understand foreign tax forms—and then as an assistant editor at Grand Central Publishing. In that position, I actually worked on business books, but it always felt ironic. "I'm still not really sure what money is," I would tell my boss. While there, I certainly learned things I might not have known, both from my boss and those books, but I generally still preferred to pitch ideas like *Black Widow-ing for Fun and Profit*. While an enthusiastic editor, I stayed a fundamentally un-businesslike person.

At my next job, as a features editor for a blog network, I signed correspondence "xoxo business <3" and wooed writers with subject lines like, "LET ME PAY YOU MONEY $$$." Now I'm a freelance writer, a notoriously business-oriented profession that allows me to watch Kathy Lee and Hoda at the gym. But I of all people have a business partner. And without her I would really be a joke.

In the summer of 2013, my friend (and at the time, co-worker) Allyson Rudolph and I founded The League of Assistant Editors, a professional networking group for agents and editors in book publishing. At the time, we were both assistant editors at GCP, and we had been fast friends with heavily overlapping lives since Allyson started at the imprint earlier that year. As industry nerds, we talked a lot about our various frustrations with and ideas about publishing at large, and the things we wanted for our own careers. Namely, we wanted to buy more books.

We knew we shared a problem with our fellow assistant editors: We found it hard to meet and get to know new agents, agents who could sell us new and exciting books. It seemed like a silly problem because it grew out of the weird opacity that characterizes book publishing, which runs on a system of knowing—but mostly being known by—agents. Silly, but solvable. We believed agents would want to meet us, if only they knew about our minimal but still existing budgets and intense desire to buy books. We were young and we were hungry. We wanted a place at the table, even if we had to set those tables up ourselves.

One night, the assistants of GCP were out for drinks, celebrating someone or something, as we always were, and Allyson told me her fantastic idea: speed-networking events. They would be just like speed-dating, but for agents and editors to meet and discuss their lists in a concentrated, fun space. I, in turn, had the fantastic idea of ordering more wine and haranguing Allyson about what a good idea this was.

We all had lots of ideas around then, especially during celebrations, but this one felt different. It felt important but attainable, necessary and actionable, so I did my part: I refused to let it drop, and that night we talked logistics and locations and branding and all the things that make ideas real. We talked about the things we could start off doing and the things we could dare to do. We named it. I promised to share my shoulder for whatever burdens would come up, and we both understood that this was something we were all in for.

In the next days, we just kept moving. We met with speed-dating experts to figure out what was what, and our HR department to find out what wouldn't get us fired. We confirmed a location and a ticket price, put together our social media accounts, started a newsletter, drew up a goofy logo, and sent out press releases. We did media interviews in the conference room, running around to let our colleagues know that—NO BIG DEAL—we were being profiled for our own ideas. We mapped out our tables, giving each one an adorable title, and ordered special pencils with our business name—The League—on them. When the tickets went live, all seventy-six sold out in a matter of days.

In September of 2013 we held our first event at Housing Works in Manhattan. Book deals were made, all the proceeds went to charity, and despite the fact that no couples actually met cute at our first event (allowing us to write and sell a romantic comedy called "Speed Pitch"), we were a huge success. And a few weeks later, I left book publishing.

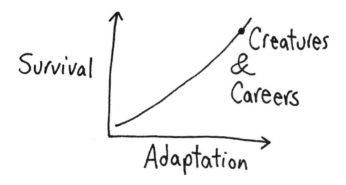

Contrary to how it all might sound, I didn't leave book publishing in *spite* of The League. In fact, my connection and continued dedication to the group made me feel like I wouldn't have to fully leave the incredibly maddening industry that I stupidly love. For the first time, I had a professional identity that didn't hinge on who had hired me or where I worked or what I had been allowed to buy; it came from something I had helped to build. When I was scared or apprehensive about something at my new job, which paid better and involved more responsibility than my previous position, I thought about those assembled agents and editors, moving every three minutes to the ding of our bell.

Since that first event, Allyson and I have put on four League events, each one better than the last. But that's not the end of what our business partnership has come to mean. For one thing, we served together as programming co-chairs for BinderCon, a symposium for female and gender-non-conforming writers, and coordinated panels featuring badass women like Jill Abramson, Anna Holmes, Amanda Hess, Jenna Wortham, and more.

We've moved on in our careers—Allyson has become a full-time editor for Overlook Press, and I stopped lying about "just wanting to edit" and started gathering bylines of my own—but when we have ideas, we know where to go. Whether it's a book idea or a new website or an app that scrapes the Susan Miller horoscope for dates to put in your calendar, we're one another's first gut check.

It's hard to say exactly why our collaborating works well for us. It's not quite as simple as having different strengths—while we're far from identical, we're both small, voicey women who like having and executing ideas—but it might be that we have those different strengths at different times. In our work, we keep each other moving. If one of us knows some aspect of a project intimidates or overwhelms the other, the other person tries to step up. When things get too intense, we give each other a break.

Thinking of our friendship as a business partnership makes me feel more responsible, not only to Allyson but also to myself. It's more than just being buddies with a co-worker or having a friend whom you can vent to about work; it's also knowing you have someone who is going to be working with you after the work is over. It's knowing you have someone else who thinks the work is worth doing.

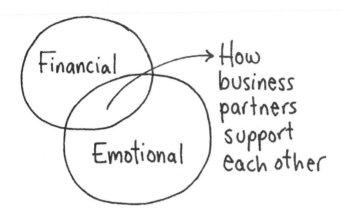

I'm still not a numbers gal, so I won't try to count how many times our partnership kept me going after the kind of setback that would have made me quit a solo project. I just know that I am unwilling to let Allyson down. Just like doing my own taxes, it's impossible to quantify what bravery our partnership has lent me. I have been able to better honor my own instincts and aspirations because of the way she has treated them. I have taken myself more seriously because I take her seriously. I have learned to do business because there is business that needs to be done. And along with my partner, I'm the business human who is going to make it happen.

Act on This

Who is your partner in crime?
Your work spouse?
Your confidant?

✳ ✳ ✳

If you're not officially working on a side project
together, now is the time to start.

✳ ✳ ✳

Rip this page out and hand it to them.

✳ ✳ ✳

Get together and begin plotting: The world needs
dominating, and you two are just the ones to do it.

Lessons for the Hustle Economy from the Frontiers of Battle Rap and Game Design

ALEX LARSEN (AKA KID TWIST),
BATTLE RAPPER AND GAME DESIGNER

Lesson 1: Thought Out > Freestyled

When I tell people that I'm a game designer, the first question I usually get is a half-joking, "So you just play games all day, right?" When I tell them that I'm also a battle rapper, their first question (or possibly second, after "You mean like in *8 Mile*?") is a more serious, "So you just make it all up as you go, right?"

The short answer to both questions is: Uh, no. The longer answers are less dismissive, but the full story doesn't offer much clarity, just a richer confusion.

"Game designer" is, first of all, a somewhat nebulous term even inside the games industry. It can involve everything from tweaking the numbers that control a level's physics to fleshing out the backstory of a world. Any decision that will affect the player's end experience is a design decision.

In its simplest and most maddening terms, a game designer's job is to make the game fun. This is a serious task when your toes are on the starting line of a multi-year development cycle costing tens of millions of dollars. It requires laying out a clear vision of what the final product will be and then constantly adjusting that vision to hit the numerous moving targets of timeline, budget, and business objectives (the latter is generally code for "demands from a manager who doesn't know shit about games").

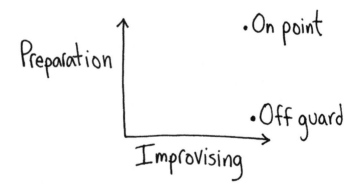

The myth of all rap battles being "freestyled" is a bit harder to tackle. Even many hip-hop fans are unaware that the word "freestyle" itself has a fuzzy and contentious meaning, especially on the East Coast. Novitiates tend to think that it necessarily signals an improvisation, but it can also refer to rapping a written verse either a capella or over a beat it wasn't intended for, a definition that goes back to the beginning of the genre. And even in pure "freestyle battles," the top performers always use what we call premeds, short for "premeditated rhymes," a softer term than outright accusing someone of spitting writtens.

What really changed the game was YouTube.

As soon as the site launched, battle fans began uploading the grainy camcorder videos they had been hoarding and trading on rap forums for years. Suddenly, everyone knew what everyone else looked like. Given how small the local scenes were, it was easy to get an idea of who would be at a given event and then show up with lines written specifically for them. And not only did YouTube kill freestyling, it also killed beats and stages and mics. It was easier to put out a good product on video in the rawer street battle format; you didn't need a venue or large crew or even permits if you knew the right spots to shoot. The combination of technological possibility and mass popularity have made a capella written battles the dominant format, with battle rap leagues all over the world getting YouTube views that reach into the millions.

Game designer. Battle rapper. The other common response I get when someone learns about my parallel careers is some mention of just how *strange* the game design/battle rap amalgam seems. But, in my experience, this kind of unrestrained boundary crossing is the rule, not the exception; I have yet to meet a creative person my age or younger who isn't also a polymath of some sort. And while the Internet enables and encourages such hybridization, it also turns creative communities into airtight echo chambers, with more acronyms, jargon, and in-jokes than any one person can reasonably learn.

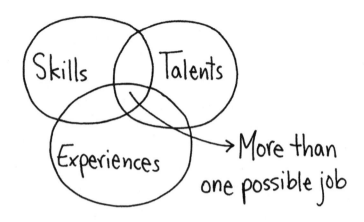

Which means, I'm sure, that the game designers I know who are also coders, tech journalists, screenwriters, cartoonists, and illustrators, and the rappers who are also actors, sketch comedians, painters, and poets, are all constantly clearing up misconceptions about their own varied pursuits, with answers that are equally complex and unsatisfying.

Lesson 2: Teams > Visionaries

The phrase "Hustle Economy" tends to imply a lone creator starting up a million-dollar media empire from a laptop in her bedroom. Just as often, though, it manifests as a large company hustling to understand and exploit an online space before its competitors do the same. And more capital can mean more potential for success—or sweepingly theatrical failure.

I've personally witnessed the latter case twice: Once at Ganz, the company behind the massively successful children's game *Webkinz*, and once at JumpOff, the first outlet to host a truly worldwide rap battle tournament. "Ganz" and "JumpOff" might not mean much to the average person, but for anyone in their respective industries, these single words hold an instant significance that is comparable to, say, "Chernobyl."

People who will watch you fail or win (y-axis)

Hype (x-axis)

Ganz started out as a family-run manufacturer of homey gifts and dollar-store tchotchkes—decidedly not a video game company. By the time I was hired, the founder's grandson Howard Ganz had taken over the reins. *Webkinz* was Howard's big gamble. What if, he posited, each plush toy gave kids access to an online world, where they could play with and care for a virtual version of their new pet?

Today, this seems obvious, but *Webkinz* was the first to get there. The most unexpected outcome of *Webkinz*'s stratospheric growth was the huge number of *adults* who were playing. Howard realized that if he could market a product directly to this market—mostly 40+ women, a demographic the games industry had outright ignored to that point—there was big money to be made. He envisioned our next project as a full-scale MMO, the *World of Warcraft* for middle-aged, middle-American women. And he wanted us to build it in nine months.

If anyone in upper management had actually been involved in developing an MMO before, they would have laughed Howard out of his own office at that timeline. But they hadn't. One PM who arrived close to the end told me, "I've read about projects like this in books." He didn't mean as an example to be followed.

Even before that particular project was shut down without producing so much as a playable build, four new games of similar scope were already underway. They, at least, made it out the door, but not much further. I followed them shortly afterward. Today, after years of losses and steady layoffs, the staff that used to fill six rooms' worth of converted warehouse space now fits in half of one room. All of the managers responsible are still there, of course.

JumpOff's rise and fall in the battle world was characterized by the opposite mistake: bringing in the *right* people and then *not* listening to them, to the point of outright disrespect. Which is a certain death sentence in a context where street rules are only one step removed.

The owner of JumpOff was a smooth-headed Brit known by the always-ironic, now-infamous mononym Harry. To his credit, the concept of a global battle league was nothing short of visionary at the time, and he believed so boldly in its potential that he sold his London flat to finance it.

The World Rap Championships was organized as a two-versus-two competition, with divisions in Toronto, the UK, Australia, and all over the States. I partnered with another rapper I knew through a mutual friend, named PORICH (derived from "Poor Rich"—stylization his). After winning the Toronto division, Rich and I moved on to the playoffs in New York.

This is where shit really popped off. The WRCs had been plagued all along by dubious judging calls. Finally, a member of the Detroit team thought to confer directly with the judges after a questionable loss in the semifinals. It turned out they had each written down a different result than the one Harry announced. I remember walking into the hallway to see the judging panel of Craig G., Pumpkinhead, and Poison Pen—all rappers with hot-forged respect and all New Yorkers of significant size—speaking to Harry in fuck-you tones, and explicitly thinking that I was witnessing the end of JumpOff.

I was more right than I knew. A few rounds later, after some frantic scuffling around the table in the corner, Harry called our attention to admit, "We've, uh, misplaced the tapes. All of them." Hours of searching, including bag-checks and pat-downs, turned up nothing. The rest of the battles went ahead, but with only B-roll footage to show for most of the tournament. JumpOff no longer had a viable online product. From that anticlimactic moment on, the company was essentially a nonfactor.

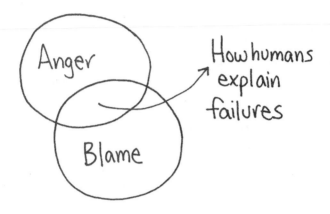

The mystery of what happened to the JumpOff tapes has passed into battle rap urban legend. The leading theory is that the Detroit team or one of their entourage stole them in retribution, which the two rappers themselves have at various times both confirmed and denied. It's also possible one or more of the judges were involved, or that JumpOff themselves messed up the footage and were trying to cover their asses.

Despite being antipodal as organizations, JumpOff and Ganz degenerated into similar cautionary tales about what happens when a sole benefactor pushes too hard into a space he doesn't truly understand. But they also each gave a vast cross-section of like-minded creative people a unique chance to connect. The crop of battle leagues that now run the scene were almost all founded by former WRC entrants, including the Toronto-based King of the Dot—one of the largest battle organizations in the world—whose first event was headlined by PORICH and myself. And I was brought in to my current game design job by a friend I met at Ganz; there are similar pockets of ex-Ganzers at gaming and animation companies all over the city.

This is by far the most exciting aspect of working in the modern economy. Creative pursuits—even those as ego-driven as battle rap—are, in the end, necessarily collaborative. And you can never predict just where those collaborations might come from, or how far they might take you.

Lesson 3: Sanity > Success

I was twenty-five years old when I started experiencing anxiety attacks for the first time. Exclusively at the office. I would retreat to whichever lounge area or washroom stall I found empty and try to calm my breathing. Sometimes it worked.

The pressure reached its worst point when I booked a battle at what would be King of the Dot's biggest event yet. What I didn't realize is that, the week before the battle, my current project at Ganz would be going into Crunch. This is an infamous games industry term for the standard period before launch when the team works unpaid overtime—evenings, weekends, all-nighters, whatever it takes—in order to make the deadline. We had already passed by several arbitrary "launch dates" for the game with no consequence, but for whatever reason, the powers-that-be decided we were going to make *this* one. (We didn't.)

Work

Play

When your hobbies are revenue streams

That event set a record for KOTD attendance. I could barely move through the crowd in the one-room club; I could not move the cement block that was sitting on top of my chest. I'd had no time for sleep in the past seven days, let alone editing and practicing my verses to the expected level. Not only did my opponent rip me apart in what I consider the worst loss I've ever taken, but I got my first taste of the morning-after Twitter backlash. Now that everyone had an image to maintain and a visible public platform on which to do so, the battle wasn't over when you left the ring.

There was even more social media anxiety to contend with at Ganz. After we finally managed to launch a game, I was responsible for interacting with our new fans over Facebook—an overwhelming task, even with our modest install base. I created an admin account and accepted friend requests so they could message me, which meant that I saw semi-frequent posts in my newsfeed about another player losing their house, or going bankrupt from medical bills. Our game was free to play; we made money only through selling access to special "premium" items. Essentially, people were spending money for pixels on a screen, and some of them were spending in the hundreds.

We had tools that would have let me check for any crossover between the bankruptcies and the big spenders. But I never had the stomach to do it.

Then, there were the other stories. Two of our most-involved fans lived in Romania, a mother and her school-aged daughter. They became so close with the game community that the daughter started referring to one of the older women—a Canadian who had emigrated from Ecuador—as "grandma." The daughter posted her report card and got an instant stream of congratulatory comments. And when we did a live fan chat event, we received a long private message from one player telling us that no matter how many bugs or issues there were with the game, she would always keep playing, because the community had given her a sense of belonging that she hadn't felt since her husband passed. A few of us might have had to wipe tears off our keyboards that night.

Contradictory as it may seem, this surreal unifying pull is very much part of the battle scene as well, although for a different generation and gender. I will never forget standing in the entrance of the club at one of KOTD's marquee World Domination events, for which battlers fly in from across the globe, and being told by a Filipino rapper that I was a big influence on him—right before a passing Norwegian joined the conversation to tell me the same.

What I came to realize is: In the Hustle Economy, whatever your job title may be, your most critical task is the management of your own anxiety. Stress is a constant presence in any hustle-based industry, and it only increases with time and success. Finding strategies to cope is a matter of sheer survival.

In the case of battle rap, I eventually had to stop logging into my pseudonymous accounts altogether. Sustained existence in that world was just too much. And contrary to conventional wisdom, my name was not forgotten when I stopped tweeting every minute. I haven't battled in more than two years, and I still get recognized in public; I've had some long, rewarding conversations this way, even in Real Life.

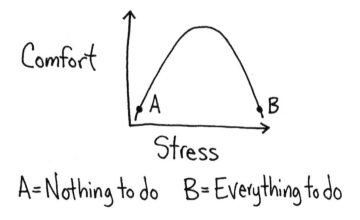

Perhaps what has helped the most, though, is the thought that the crushing anxiety inherent to the Hustle Economy is a necessary counterpart to its addictive vital energy. My favorite battle line ever directed at me was from a rapper named 100 Bulletz: "How're you an atheist, but don't believe in evolution?" His use of my personal views to skewer my battle career's stagnation was gleefully devastating. But taking the line seriously, Bulletz was exactly wrong. Evolution is one of the few things I *do* believe in.

And it's the energy of evolution, sped up, that drives the creative hustle—reckless, full of impropriety, coursing ceaselessly, and striving in every direction to find a way forward.

Act on This

Zoom in on the source of your stress.

* * *

Are you anxious because you have too many
things to tackle, or not enough?

* * *

Are you focused on accomplishing things,
or merely on dealing with people?

* * *

What makes you crazy can also motivate you:
Go in the direction your stress is guiding you.

* * *

Go toward what's challenging but potentially amazing.

* * *

Get away from what's challenging but doesn't
offer you any pay-offs.

Eat What You Want; Leave What You Don't

NANCY ZASTUDIL,
GALLERIST, CURATOR, AND ARTS WRITER

In September 2014, I opened my own business: an art gallery of all things, in Albuquerque, New Mexico, of all places. As I write this, my gallery is in the first month of operation, and it's scary as hell.

In addition to running the gallery, I juggle two day jobs and two or three freelance gigs on any given day. And as I hustle to meet deadlines, pay bills, stay sane, and spend quality time with my partner (who, by the way, is a major factor to making this all possible), my grandfather's advice is at the forefront of my brain.

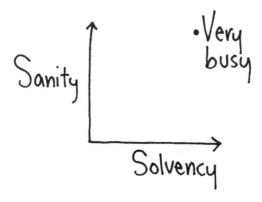

My grandfather, Harold Nestor, was an inspiration to me. Only now, as an adult, do I recognize how much. Sometimes his words come back to me at the oddest moments.

My grandfather started a technical college in the basement of a local Ohio high school, using a shoebox as his briefcase; the school went on to become Columbus State Community College. Beyond this accomplishment, he also served in the Navy, owned and operated an antique furniture store and refinishing shop, married and raised two daughters, and took his five grandchildren on epic summer vacations. He had a 1971 T-top Corvette, and he rode his motorcycle to Tennessee on the weekends, if only for breakfast. He survived numerous heart attacks in his early years and walked miles a day for exercise in his later years. Known affectionately as Purt by his friends and Bo by his grand-kids, Dr. Nestor died suddenly, on a business trip, in 1995.

Bo often took us grandkids out for nice dinners, and as children often do, we picked at our food and were "done" with more than half of our servings still on the plate. Faced with impatient and squirrelly kids, in fancy expensive restaurants in big cities, he often said to us, in a very matter-of-fact way, "Eat what you want; leave what you don't."

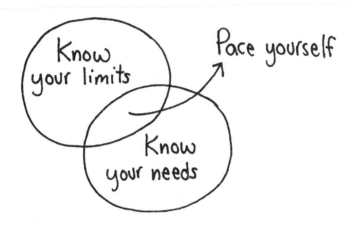

He never forced us to clean our plates and never shamed us for being wasteful (or maybe he just wanted to avoid causing a scene). Bo had plenty of money to spend on us fickle kids, money for which he worked very hard, long hours. He could have forced us to sit and finish the food in front of us; he could have lectured us about being thankful for what we have, to remember those who had less, etc., etc. Instead, the occasional "your eyes are bigger than your stomach" comment gently reminded us that, next time, we should be more thoughtful about what we chose to order and/or more determined in our eating.

While the suggestion "eat what you want; leave what you don't" might, at first glance, seem like a flippant and self-centered resolve, with little-to-no regard for expense, there is a truism that rings at a deeper level for me. In essence I hear: Do what you want. And of course, the cliché quickly follows: To thine own self be true.

In other words, don't force yourself to do, or partake, or be force-fed anything that does not whet your appetite, tempt your palate, fit your tastes, or intrigue, entice, or otherwise nourish you.

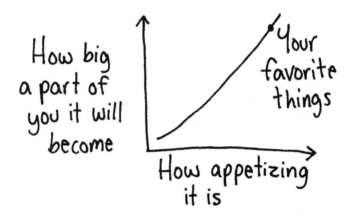

And finally, don't overdo it. The bottom line is to do what you want, no matter what that is, as long as it doesn't hurt the people or places around you. Try something new—you just might go back for more. This is as true for the arts as it is for any other nourishment.

Trust your gut—and your tastes.

Act on This

Hunger is an honest feeling. Listening to it will help
you discover what you really want.

***

Admit that you are greedy and ravenous.
Make no apologies for your hunger.
Make no attempts to minimize that feeling.

***

In three sentences or fewer, describe your greediest
dream: the ultimate feast for your soul.

***

You're one step closer to it, now that you
can see it in all of its mouthwatering glory.
Now go make it happen.

The Long Bet

LE LEFEVER,
COFOUNDER AND CREATIVE DIRECTOR
OF COMMON CRAFT

Here's a riddle: Your ability to be successful can hinge on this idea. You must earn it, but you can't save or spend it. Once you have it, the battle begins to maintain it. But the passage of time always takes it away. What is it?

The answer: Relevance; having current and practical social importance.

Actor and author B.J. Novak summed it up nicely in this tweet: "Some people have fuck-you money but nobody has fuck-you relevance."

It's so true. Relevance is slippery. The moment your work becomes a part of the zeitgeist, the moment that what you have to say matters, that relevance can slip away. No matter how relevant you become, it will vanish unless you consistently find new ways to replenish it. And that requires hustle.

A Brush with Relevance

My first bit of relevance came through the work of my company, Common Craft. My wife Sachi and I made a handful of animated videos in 2007 that explained ideas like RSS, wikis, and blogs "in plain English." These videos went on to become viral hits in the early days of YouTube and are now known as the first animated explainer videos.

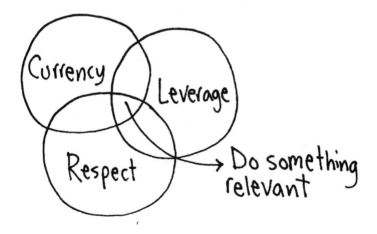

Just days after we published the first video, everything started to change. Our inboxes became full of offers, and for a while nearly everything we did seemed to get attention. The videos were getting thousands of views a day and appearing on the front page of Digg.com. This took us by surprise; we never guessed the videos would be so popular. It was intoxicating.

Soon enough we were being hired by companies like LEGO, Google, Dropbox, and Ford to explain their products and services. Our newfound relevance was translating into a successful business. Despite having little experience with what we were doing, we were now professional producers.

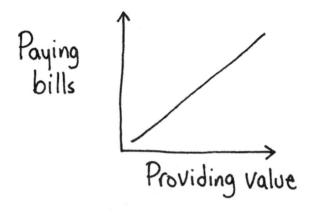

While these custom video projects paid the bills, we continued to make educational videos like our first ones. These videos, what we considered the *real* Common Craft videos, continued to be a big priority despite producing little income. They were about *ideas* and not products.

We Earned It! Now What?

For the first couple of years, we were so busy that we hardly had time to think about where we were headed. New leads arrived every day. We were working like we'd never worked before.

We learned some valuable lessons in those early days. First, we loved the idea that the two of us, a married couple, could make a living by making animated videos. We didn't require a big studio or other producers or actors. We were a self-contained creative unit based from our home in Seattle.

Over time, this aspect of Common Craft became paramount. We loved our jobs and the lifestyle it enabled. We had stumbled onto an opportunity of a lifetime, something that meant we could have absolute freedom from regular corporate jobs. The question became: How can we make this last? How can we keep doing this for another decade or more?

While we were at the height of our relevance, an idea crept into our consciousness. We started to see the custom video part of our business a little differently. It was a part of the promotional media world, an industry that is prone to short-term fads. The cool new thing today could quickly become a joke tomorrow. If this happened to us, if our signature style went out of fashion, we'd be stuck. Time could very easily take its toll on our relevance, and with it, our perfect jobs.

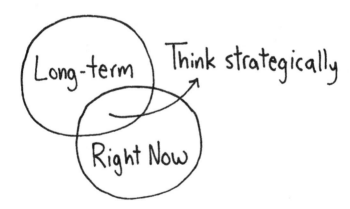

For the first time, we started to consider shaking the Etch A Sketch. Rather than watching helplessly as things changed, we decided to push the change ourselves. The question became: How can Common Craft videos have more timeless relevance?

The Sleepers Awaken

Since the first video in 2007, our library of educational videos continued to grow on a monthly basis. Now that we had dozens of videos, a new kind of request started to appear. It became clear to us that our videos were becoming an important tool for educators. They were solving problems and helping professionals do their jobs more effectively. These professionals began to ask us: Can I use this in my classroom? Can we use this on our intranet or in presentations? Can I download the video files?

These requests triggered ideas. People were prepared to license our work, to pay for permission to use them professionally. We saw that the educational videos, unlike the custom ones, could be produced once and licensed multiple times, like software. Could we turn our videos into a product?

A Big Decision

Sachi and I did not take this potential opportunity lightly. To make the licensing model work, we needed to make it our primary focus and work to build relevance within a completely new niche.

Would we abandon our current success in order to focus on licensing, something that was just a possibility? Were we willing to trade custom video revenue today for the potential of passive, scalable revenue in the future? It was an agonizing decision—our future hung in the balance.

Along the way, we learned a few things about the educational media industry. First, there is an established culture of paying for educational content. Second, educational content can be virtually timeless. One video can be relevant for many years. This seemed like a near perfect way to think about the potential of our videos.

So we started testing. We offered digital downloads of "presentation quality" videos on CommonCraft.com and sold our first video within a few hours of going live. The evidence looked positive.

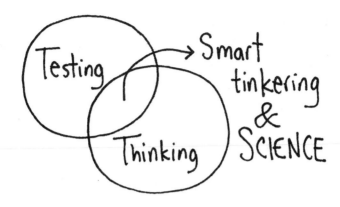

Within a few months, the decision was final. We would give up nearly everything that established our current relevance to change course. We would take ourselves out of the custom video market, stop using YouTube, and focus exclusively on licensing videos on CommonCraft.com. We were ready for the consequences.

Winding It Down, Then Slightly Up

The change started by saying "no" more often. We said no to great companies and potentially great projects. Over time, we took on fewer and fewer custom projects and oriented our website around e-commerce.

As expected, our revenue and relevance in the promotional video industry gradually fell month after month. Our licensing model was working, but it was nowhere near custom video levels. We knew it was a long bet. It might take years to achieve the relevance we needed in the educational world. And this made us study, strategize, and work even harder.

In 2012, we virtually eliminated our custom work, focused everything on licensing videos through Common Craft, and wrote a book called *The Art of Explanation*. That's where we are today. Common Craft now has individual, school, and corporate members in over fifty countries, and we remain a two-person, home-based business. The business supports us, and we feel we're just getting started, again.

A Different Kind of Relevance

These days, I think differently about what it means to be relevant. While B.J. Novak says no one has fuck-you relevance, I now believe it is possible to make relevance more sustainable. By taking risks and thinking long-term, it is possible to find niches and opportunities that can make relevance more manageable.

We made a decision to give up much of what we had achieved early on to make a long-term bet. That bet meant trading short-term success and high-profile relevance for a more focused, sustainable kind of relevance.

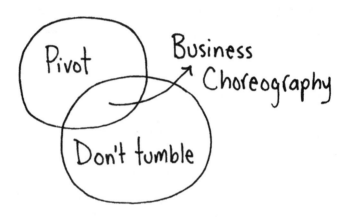

Today, our bet is still in play. We have growing relevance to those who are interested in educating others. In this niche, our content is useful, which helps our social and practical importance become more timeless. Our revenue isn't what it was at its peak, but the curve is sloping upward with each month. It's working, gradually.

Taking this leap required a commitment. Common Craft isn't just our business—it's our entire lives. This is the heart of why we were prepared to take the risk. We found something we loved, and more than anything, we wanted to continue it for years and years. So, we had to find a different kind of relevance.

Act on This

Column A: all the things you're good at.
Column B: all the things you can earn money doing.

* * *

What's in both columns? Those are your
sweet spots.

* * *

Now, take both column items and future-proof them.

* * *

How can your efforts bring you returns if media,
technology, geography, or corporate structures change?

* * *

Work toward and focus on those future states,
and you'll stay relevant.

You're Going to Get Tired
of Swimming Upstream

JEFF WYSAKI,
BLOGGER AND HUMORIST

My wife and I both willingly hurled ourselves from the comfort of the corporate work ship years ago. When we first started, my father-in-law was supportive and wished us luck. However, he also had the temerity to divine, "You're going to get tired of swimming upstream." In our youthful recklessness, we rolled our eyes at this old-world viewpoint, but in the back of my mind I feared he might be right.

I knew it then, and you probably know it now: Striking out on your own is a thousand times more difficult than settling into a traditional job. In fact, this may be the single biggest realization that's keeping you from jumping into the cold, murky waters of career insecurity.

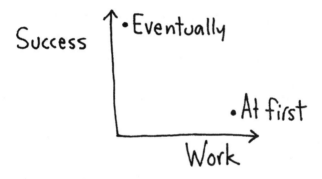

I wish I could tell you this fact is wrong; that there is, in fact, a magical way to shortcut past that upstream swim and skip right to the reward of all that sweet, steamy fish sex (er, I mean independent job success). Unfortunately, I can't do that. However, I can tell you that it will not be difficult forever. You see—and here's where my father-in-law's logic falters—it's not an upstream swim FOREVER. At some point, that current pushing you back will slow . . . then stop . . . then change course altogether. One day, you'll wake up and realize that you're finally coasting downstream in a career you forged all by yourself. It happened for me. It happened for my wife. And it can happen for you.

. . . But first, you must struggle.

On that fateful first day that I figuratively decided to flip off the corporate world, I knew I wanted three things:

1. A career that allowed me to be funny for a living.
2. The freedom to work for myself.
3. One of those cool Japanese robot dogs. You know, the ones that can bark and do backflips?

After promptly acquiring the dog, I set to work on the first two. But how do you start your career in a creative field when you have no connections and no idea what you're doing? Well, I found advice—and my compass—in what would quickly become my favorite quote: "Be so good they can't ignore you." This simple sentence, uttered by legendary comedian Steve Martin, is really the only advice anyone needs to succeed in the career path of his or her choosing. Whatever you want to do, do it hard, and do it better than anyone else. Eventually, you will get noticed.

Since the Internet was the most accessible option for getting my work seen, I created a website and started posting funny things that I made to it. Not occasionally. Or on the weekends. Or when the mood struck. EVERY DAY. I made a personal challenge to myself to create one funny thing a day, and I stuck to it. Even when no one was reading, I forced myself to work—because if you want it to be your job in the future, you have to treat it like a job right now.

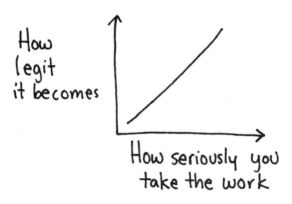

Sure, a lot of those early things I made were terrible, but the more I worked, the better I got. If I made something I thought was especially good, I sent it to larger websites. If they liked it, they'd post it. Eventually, some of them started following my work on their own. Success! I no longer had to beg them to post my work; they started doing it on their own. I thanked them. I talked to them. I found other people making things like me.

We supported and shared each other's work. With each new connection I made, that stream started to get a little less difficult to swim against.

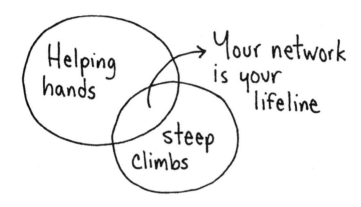

I worked hard those early years. Beyond making my own things, I started collecting and posting other funny things I found across the web. I saw what other larger humor sites were doing, and I did it better. I built up my Facebook following. And wrote jokes. And made powerful friends on Tumblr. And drew comics. And I did it all while scraping by as a freelance writer mindlessly typing out SEO articles about vasectomies and after-market car parts (among other, less terrible topics).

In total, I probably worked fifty to sixty hours each week. I worked Saturdays and sometimes Sundays. It was exhausting, but it was also worth it. Eventually, I started earning enough ad revenue off my website to quit freelancing. I'd done it: I was making people laugh, I was doing it from the comfort of my own home, and I was getting paid for it.

As time passed, my workload was streamlined. Less and less time was needed to promote myself and my blog. I was able to focus solely on finding and creating funny things. At some point along the way, I'd swam so far upstream that it changed direction. I'd started coasting.

My job is now an easy routine—and it is amazing. And because I worked so hard those early years, I have been rewarded with a job I love and a life that requires a dress shirt on very few occasions.

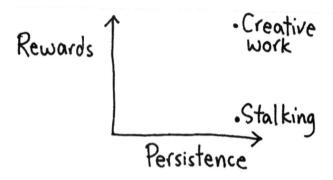

It is a dream life, and if you have the persistence to swim upstream for just a little while, it can be your life, too.

Now, if you will please excuse me. My robot dog is barking, and he needs to be fed.

Act on This

Embrace this cycle: If you feel like you are struggling, accept that this will pass, and keep working.

* * *

If you feel like you are finally successful, like you've really made it, accept that this will pass, and challenge yourself so dramatically that you can struggle again.

It's Important to Throw Things Away

JESSICA HAGY,
ARTIST AND WRITER

Stop hoarding your junk.

The vast majority of things you make are not going to be successful. Maybe they're lovely. Maybe they're heartfelt. Maybe they make you smile. Maybe you put a lot of work into them. But not everything you create is precious. Think of your output like sea turtle procreation. Out of 20,000 little turtle babies, only a handful makes it to adulthood. To a sea turtle, that's a successful percentage.

When in doubt, start over.

You can't be precious about your work. You can't cling to a novel that no editor wants. Throw it away. Write another one. You can't get angry if the world doesn't declare you a genius for a set of paintings. Throw them away. Paint new ones. You can't take it personally if no one downloads your music. Throw it away. Write new songs. You only truly fail when you stop making work. Let those tiny turtle babies go, and if all of the stars align for you, a few of them will survive.

You're always still learning.

A great, great deal of your work was just practice, anyway. The work you're doing now is just practice for the work you'll do ten years from now. Kids begin by scribbling. Then they get to stick figures. Then they scrawl out some clumsy landscapes. Kids don't give up the crayons before they reach kindergarten. They move on. They try again. They try something new. Picture yourself as a kid who is making a pile of things. And know that you always have far further to go than you have already come—no matter where you are in your career.

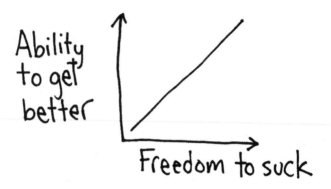

Make room for the next bigger, better thing.

By abandoning what doesn't work, you give yourself the time, freedom, and space to make more and better things. Every next thing will be better than what you did before, if you can be honest about what was good and what wasn't about your previous work. You don't stay in a relationship, a job, or a place that isn't working for you. The same is true for your work. If something isn't working, if it's not rewarding, if no one cares, move the heck on.

Let the good stuff go, too.

Even if your last piece was a smashing success, you can still do better. You can always do better. Use the revenue from your last success to fund your next project. Throw away what you already did, and move on. If sharks stop swimming, they die. Be a shark. Sharks are powerful, sexy, and intimidatingly fierce. Keep swimming. The faster you can let go of the old and begin the new, the faster you improve. Remember: You cannot hold a toxic grudge against yourself—you must let your work evolve, and forgive yourself for past misadventures.

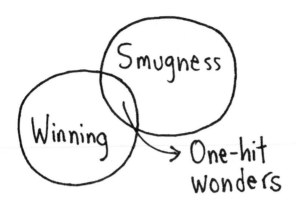

Smugness

Winning

→ One-hit wonders

Go places by dropping your baggage.

Throwing out the old stuff will transform the kind of artist you are. Making new and different work, every piece of it, makes you less bitter, less unknown, less stuck. You will have a larger, more interesting, more complex body of work. You will feel more inspired and less trapped. Clinging to past exercises is the sure path to seething depression. If you've spent any time around artists, you've seen this. If your only hope of success is that someone, somewhere, somehow, will discover and champion that thing you did three years ago, well, you're probably miserable and you're most certainly delusional. Throw it out. Make something new. Let. It. Go.

Critics can help if you know how to hear them.

Critiques can sting, or they can strengthen. Know what kind of feedback to throw out, too. A good critique will give you new routes to ponder, new ideas to play with, and point out mistakes you can correct. If you have spinach in your teeth, floss. A useless critique is just someone ranting at you, and it's probably less about your work than it is about the critic. And nagging voices aren't just other people. The voice in your head that belittles or berates you? You'll shut it up when you prove it wrong, and the only way to prove it wrong is to do more, better, bolder, more wonderful work. That'll show everybody, actually.

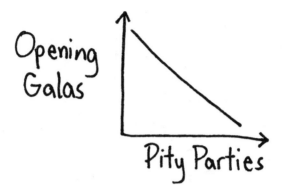

Opening Galas / Pity Parties

Surrender is not an option.

Your reaction to a piece that simply doesn't work says more about your viability as an artist than anything else. When you can pivot and create something better, you are the epitome of success. But on the other hand, artists who don't make art, like writers who don't write or salespeople who don't sell—that's the definition of failure. Making work that isn't your best and then moving on to something better—that's progress.

Every chore can be a creative exercise.

And it's not just the actual work. It's how you present it. It's who sees it. It's where it lives. It's whom you sell it to. Your creativity cannot be confined to your chosen medium. Your approach to your work must be as clever and inventive as the work itself. Look at your business structure. Look at your positioning. Examine your marketing and your business model. Spend a fraction of your time in the studio, producing. Spend the vast majority of your time on the business of your art. Be as creative as possible in every possible way. Throw away your clients who take more than they pay you. Throw out the artist statement that isn't strong enough. Throw out your old new-business methods. Throw out your old patterns of sales. Talk to new people whom you admire and like being around. Work on new routes to market. Change up your formats, your identities, your styles.

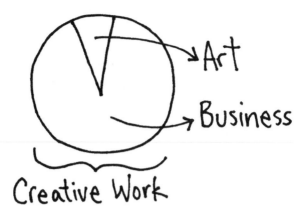

Creative Work

You can keep bits and pieces of broken things.

While you're sorting through your work and your approaches to it, know that it's OK to hesitate before tossing something. You're creative. You know that not everything is black and white. Some things will have redeeming qualities and horrible features. Again, use your creativity to tweak what you can, to throw out the bathwater and keep the baby (or send the baby to daycare while you paint with the bathwater; do what works best for you). Did that last article resonate on one level and flop on another? Focus on what worked, but reinvent it for the next issue. Does that gallery put on a great event but have mediocre marketing? Jump in there and change it up before your next show.

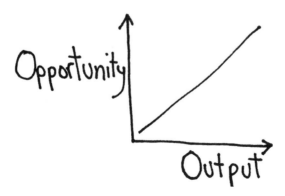

Just. Keep. Going.

Some people make a lot of things. Play with a ton of ideas. Experiment with different venues and media, different audiences and sales streams. As long as you're playing, tinkering, making—you're on the right path.

Act on This

Let something go. Let a few things go.

✳ ✳ ✳

Find some work that is weighing on you—
whether due to your relationship to it, or its relationship
to the world—and just let it go.

✳ ✳ ✳

Start working on something that is worth
working on.

You Are the Product, and the Product Sucks: Advice to an Artistic Entrepreneur

ZACH WEINERSMITH,
WEB COMIC

My dad thinks I'm a great businessman. He's probably not entirely wrong. I *do* have a business. The business has employees. I talk to a CPA a few times a year, and I have been known to consider a bunch of numbers on a spreadsheet. I occasionally get on a conference call, and sentences like, "We could do this cheaper in China" are used.

But, secretly, I'm terrible at business. I have learned to do it out of sheer necessity. It's possible this is true of many small business owners, but I'm convinced it's especially true for me. I have reluctantly learned how to design merchandise, how to source products, how to run a Facebook page and a Twitter account. But, I don't enjoy it. I don't like the cut and thrust of business. I don't experience contentment at seeing product shipped. I don't enjoy business politics or glad-handing.

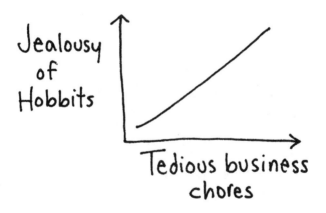

I am, in short, a Hobbit. I would be perfectly happy spending my time in a small room, reading books, ignoring the world.

As it turns out, that doesn't pay very well.

The Equation for Success

So, I've had to strategize. I want to put forth a very simple equation to explain what my strategy has been:

$$S = P \times A$$

S = probability of success
P = the product
A = all the crap you do to get people to care about P

I am not naturally good at A. I've become better at it over time, but it will never be a very high number. So, my best bet is to try to max out P.

Here's the tricky part: I'm an artist by trade. I *am* the product. How do I make *me* better?

Here's the part where a lot of people might give you some motivational bilge about how "you can do it!" I'm not really into that. Maybe you can't do it. I don't know you. All I can say is this: Once you've realized that, yes, the product is YOU, it's time to think hard about making the product suck less.

Making the Product Suck Less

In my case, my strategy has been to make the product know more than its consumers. Here's what that entails:

1. Read. A lot.
   My minimum is three books a week. In a good week, I might get closer to six or seven, depending on how thick the books are and what I'm up to in terms of projects.

2. Read diversely.
   No, science fiction AND fantasy is not diverse reading. Go get a book that's boring. Be bored while you read it. What's that? You don't *like* being bored? So what? I don't like that I have to exercise to keep fit.

3. Don't read what everyone else is reading.

I'm a cartoonist. On my stack of books to read there are exactly zero comic books. Here are a few books that are in my pile: *The Oxford Handbook of Maritime Archaeology*; *The Social Biology of Ropalidia Marginata*; *Summa Technologiae*; *The English and Scottish Popular Ballads*; *The Autobiography of GK Chesterton*.

Why am I reading these books? BECAUSE YOU AREN'T. OK, maritime archaeology sounds cool, but the rest of it will contain a lot of boring content. I will still read every word. Because you won't. My job as an entertainer is to be more interesting than you. I figure that leaves two choices: know a bunch of weird stuff, or go on a wild and dangerous adventure. As I mentioned, I'm a Hobbit.

4. Be boring.

When you go to a great concert, do you know why it's great? It's because everyone playing or singing or dancing has spent a lot of time being really, really boring: playing the same song over and over, quibbling over when light number 42-B should come up, making sure every viewing angle is as good as possible. In fact, a good concert is the result of *fractal* boringness. Boring growing on boring that grew on boring. The violinist is playing an instrument that is the end result of centuries of people sitting around thinking about wood type, resin type, acoustics, mathematics of harmony, and so on.

If you want to rise to the level of that concert you loved, or book you loved, or device you loved, you need to be boring. Talking about what you're going to do doesn't make it happen. Feeling passionate about what you're going to do doesn't make it happen. Fuck your passion. You know who has passion? A teenager who just heard a One Direction song. What you need is focus and patience.

5. Schedule your life.

There are many ways to do this. I originally used a Ben Franklin style "I will do X at Y o'clock" schedule system. Later, I moved to a more freeform "do the following tasks every day, in any order" schema. But, especially if you work from home, you need to schedule your life. If you don't believe me, try writing down a work diary. Compare your accomplishments on scheduled days to unscheduled days, and you will be amazed.

6. Turn off the Internet.

Turn it off. Right now. Your job is not to browse Facebook.

The Product Might Suck More Than You Realize

In my own trade of comics, one thing I see a lot is what might be called "parabolic quality." Quality goes up, quality comes down. Often a new cartoonist will start out quite good, then be great for a few months, then stink, then finally quit. Why? Because they're using up a finite resource. They're using every clever thought, joke, conversation, or turn of phrase they ever had before doing comics. Much like petroleum, the fuel is still being created, but not nearly as fast as it gets used up.

This finite resource can lead to overconfidence. On your first day, you might have twenty good ideas. You'll think "Ah! This is easy! I could do this all day." You would be wrong.

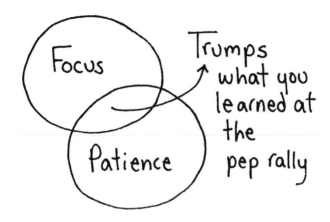

When you start in this business, you have a nice stock of comic fuel. If you don't learn to replenish as you go, you're screwed. The way I replenish as I go is outlined above. Your method might vary, but the basic concept is the same: The stuff of your creativity needs to be replenished, even if you're feeling good about your reserves today.

Making a Living

All of that stuff above is the major thing, if you're like me. Perhaps you're not like me, and you're really, really good at squeezing every penny from your business. If so, you might not have to work as hard. To my mind, the beautiful life is spent reading and thinking. My business model permits this reasonably well. Your good life may be quite different, and so your methods may vary.

That said, in terms of making a living, I do have a bit of common-sense advice: Running a business, like all things, takes mastery. The stuff you can learn out of a book could be taught in a week. Everything else is the wages of diligence. You already know that you ought to be able to use social media. You already know that you can run advertising or sell ads or put yourself on Patreon. So, with that in mind, I have one piece of advice that you might not already know. It is this: Don't assume the system is at equilibrium.

I mean that in a somewhat nerdy sense. A system is at equilibrium when it stops changing rapidly. If you pull a slinky apart and then let go, it'll wobble back and forth and back and forth, compressing and expanding, until it reaches its equilibrium and stops. In business, if you see that the same commodity is being sold at wildly varying prices, the commodity's price has not equilibrated at a particular level.

There is an old joke in economics that goes like this: An economist and a businessman are walking. They see a 100-dollar bill. The businessman bends to pick it up, at which point the economist says, "Don't bother." The businessman asks, "Why?" The economist replies, "If the system is at equilibrium, the 100-dollar bill doesn't exist."

In other words, that bill should've been picked up by now! This is clearly illogical thinking. Even if the system is roughly at equilibrium, you should occasionally find things that are way off.

Not realizing this fact was a big mistake early on for me. Here were some dumb errors I made that involve the equilibrium assumption:

1. All ad providers are the same.
   SO WRONG. I think it was in 2007 or so that I switched one provider and basically doubled my income. This shouldn't be the case, since the providers are buying the same stuff! But, it is the case. I should've switched much sooner.

2. All merchandise is the same.
   Maybe one shirt is more popular than another, but there's no way there's THAT much variance. Right? SO WRONG. I have had designs that sell about a dozen copies, and other designs that sell 1,000 in the first week! Some stuff hits. Some stuff doesn't. It's hard to predict. But don't assume that you just put out stuff and make money. You have to put out the right stuff.

3. You do your work and get your audience based on how good your work is.

   There is truth to this, but it's way more complicated. You need to network and interact. My comic was doing well, but didn't take off until I started meeting peers and doing guest comics. I hate networking, but it matters. So do it.

4. Little stuff doesn't matter.

   WRONG. For example, recently we finally started properly running our Facebook group. It has more members than our daily on-site viewership. This may take from site traffic a little, *but* it also means we sell a lot more merchandise.

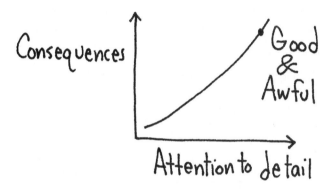

The Equation Revisited

In sum: Don't assume things are at equilibrium. You might be leaving money on the table. Remember the equation above: $S = P \times A$.

If you've got Product really, really high, a small change in A will make a big difference. If you have a big audience that loves what you're doing, they will WANT to pay for your content. You just need to give them the way to do it.

The Most Important Advice

1. Be patient.

   This will probably take years. It may take a decade. From the time I started actively trying to make a living at comics, it took about three years. It took an additional five or so years after that before I made a good living. You are building a cultural entity from air. It will take time.

2. Be diligent.

   There will be highs and lows. In my case, the great recession literally started right after the first year I made a decent wage for myself. I have no way of knowing if this was related, but my income definitely fell with the recession. Here's where diligence comes in. Your income is down, perhaps your confidence is down, but you can't stop. Keep putting in the work. The audience will appreciate it, and when the economic weather turns fair again, you will profit.

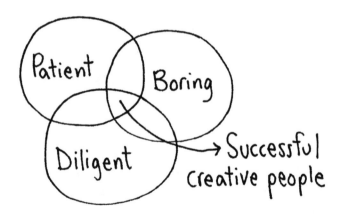

3. Be boring.

   Stop reading this essay. Go pick up a big, fat textbook. Your work will be better.

Act on This

Become intellectually omnivorous.

* * *

Feed your brain more hearty ideas.

* * *

It's time to read more broadly, more deeply,
and more frequently. Get your library card out,
or go get one if you don't have one.

* * *

You've reached the end of this book:
Now get to the end of many more.

* * *

Your work will reflect your brain's improved
diet of delicious stories.

About the Contributors

Jason Oberholtzer is a content creator, producer, and strategist whose writing, charts, GIFs, and blogs appear all over the web and in print. His clients include *Forbes*, IBM, Jazz at Lincoln Center, and the *Economist*. He founded the blog *I Love Charts* in 2009, which with over 500,000 followers remains one of Tumblr's most influential blogs. Through *I Love Charts*, he frequently collaborates with well-known bloggers and artists, and occasionally, when he's feeling especially civic-minded, the White House. *I Love Charts: The Book* was published in 2012 by Sourcebooks.

Jessica Hagy is an artist and writer best known for her Webby award–winning blog, *Indexed* (ThisIsIndexed.com). A fixture in the creative online space, Jessica has been illustrating, consulting, and speaking to international media and at events since 2006. She is the author of *The Art of War Visualized* and *How to Be Interesting*, both from Workman. Her work has been described as "deceptively simple," "undeniably brilliant," and "our favorite reason for the Internet to exist." Her commissioned work frequently appears in various web formats, galleries, books, magazines, newspapers, television outlets, and advertising campaigns.

Nick Douglas is a comedy writer in New York City. He is the former editor of the blogs *Valleywag*, *Urlesque*, and *Slacktory*. Reach him at Nick@toomuchnick.com. He'll happily watch the first thirty seconds of your comedy video.

Ben Grelle (aka The Frogman) is an Internet comedian, writer, photographer, and graphic artist. He runs the popular *TheFrogMan.me,* where he creates original content and webcomics, and posts the best stuff from around the web. He is secretly controlled by a corgi named Otis.

Adrian Sanders is the cofounder of Beacon, a service that helps journalists raise funds to tell important stories. He lives and works in Oakland, CA. Previously he helped create Backspac.es, a mobile photo-storytelling app, and VM Associates, an integration consulting firm in New York City.

Farah Khalid is a film editor, writer, traveler, and dog lover. As an editor, she travels the world and works with some of the music industry's living legends. Her personal essays have been published in numerous magazines. She lives in Brooklyn, NY, and is currently working on her first novel.

Mike Rugnetta is a Brooklyn-based composer, programmer, and performer. He is a founding member of the live, lecture-based performance art trio MemeFactory, which makes fast-paced performances about the increasingly misnamed phenomenon of "Internet Culture." He is also the writer and host of *Reasonably Sound*, a podcast distributed by the Infinite Guest Network from American Public Media about the science, culture, and theory of audio and music; and *Idea Channel*, a YouTube series where critical and philosophical concepts are applied to things in the popular culture canon. *Idea Channel* is produced by PBS Digital Studios.

Emma Koenig is the creator of *F*ck! I'm in My Twenties*, an illustrated Tumblr which spawned a book, a guided journal, and a TV version developed at NBC. Her viral video "Speed Dating" has almost 2 million views. She was a humorist for the *Times UK*, and most recently, a staff writer for *Manhattan Love Story* on ABC.

Asha Dornfest is a writer, blogger, and founder of *Parent Hacks*. *Parent Hacks* was one of *Real Simple*'s three choices for "best parenting and family blog," a Daily Beast "Beast Best" award winner, and three-time recipient of Babble's "#1 Most Useful" Top Mom Blog honor. She's the author of *Parent Hacks* and the coauthor of *Minimalist Parenting: Enjoy Modern Family Life More by Doing Less*. She lives in Portland, Oregon, with her husband, son, and daughter.

Kelsey Hanson is the founder and creative director of Vocal Creative. Formerly a designer in Starbucks Global Creative Studio, she has worked with award-winning brands and agencies across the world. Habitual line-stepper, accomplished gin drinker, and mom of two, her work has been featured in *GDUSA, CA*, the Hello Poster Show, and the Seattle Show.

Mónica Guzmán is a Sunday columnist for the *Seattle Times* and a weekly columnist for GeekWire, covering issues in digital life. She emcees Ignite Seattle, a popular grab bag and community-fueled speaker series, serves on the National Advisory Board of the Poynter Institute for Media Studies, and in 2012 joined the Seattle hub of the World Economic Forum's Global Shapers Community. A juror for the 2014 Pulitzer Prizes, Mónica contributed the closing chapter "Community As an End" to the 2013 book *The New Ethics of Journalism: Principles for the 21st Century* and is vice-chair of the SPJ Ethics Committee. She was recently named a Neiman Fellow at Harvard.

Thomas Leveritt is an oil painter who specializes in portraits; he wrote a novel called *The Exchange-Rate Between Love and Money*, which got sucked into the film industry, and then so did he; he pioneered the use of ultraviolet-wavelength video in his film *How the Sun Sees You*, and continues to experiment with new forms of imaging both digital and analogue. He lives in New York.

Casey Bowers is a copywriter and journalist living in Lancaster, Ohio. His beats include music, film, tech, travel, and modern dadding. He writes for *Flush Magazine, DiscoSalt*, and various and sundry brands and publications.

Josephine Decker is an American actor, filmmaker, and performance artist. Recently named one of *Filmmaker* magazine's 25 New Faces of Independent Film, Josephine premiered her first two narrative features, *Butter on the Latch* and *Thou Wast Mild and Lovely*, at the Berlinale Forum 2014 and theatrically in NYC.

Donna Salgado is a New York City–based dance artist specializing in performance, choreography, and teaching. She is the founder of CONTINUUM Contemporary/Ballet, a dance company creating work in the concert dance spectrum, while celebrating a spirit of dance making that is inspiring, collaborative, and progressive. She holds an MFA in Dance Performance, performed professionally with several dance companies, commissioned over ten choreographers, created twenty original ballets, is an active faculty member of three major dance institutions in NYC, co-wrote the children's book *Crafterina* with her sister, and has collaborated with composers, fashion designers, visual artists, a hair guru, and a pop star.

Alex Pearlman is a digital journalist and writer based in London, and a leading commenter on free speech issues and Internet rights. After founding a startup online magazine in college, Alex worked as a product manager and digital editor at the *Boston Globe*. Her work has appeared in the *Globe*, Boston.com, *Slate* magazine, GlobalPost, The Huffington Post, and *Lemon* magazine.

Dante Shepherd (the pseudonym of Dr. Lucas Landherr) holds a PhD in chemical engineering from Cornell University and is currently a professor at Northeastern University in Boston doing engineering education research for K-12 classrooms. His perspectives on living to the age of ninety-six have been shared with *Surviving the World* since May 2008.

Brad O'Farrell has been hustling around the startup industry since 2007. He's worked for companies like Cheezburger, TurntableFN, and YouTube. In 2009 he made the viral video Play Him Off Keyboard Cat, and in 2013, he crowdfunded a game called Story War that raised $360,000 in thirty days. He is currently developing a crowdfunding service for Reddit Inc.

Jess Kimball Leslie is a trendspotter and a writer. Her work has been featured in the Hairpin, TechCrunch, the Awl, the *Atlantic*, and many more places. She lives in New York City with her wife and son.

Meredith Haggerty is a writer and editor in Brooklyn, NY. Her writing can be seen on sites like the Hairpin, Fast Company, Vulture, Matter, and the *Daily Dot*. She most recently hosted *TLDR*, a podcast about the Internet from WNYC's *On the Media*.

Alex Larsen lives in Toronto, where he currently works as a game designer. His alter ego Kid Twist is an internationally renowned battle rapper with more than five million views on YouTube.

Nancy Zastudil is a curator, writer, and administrator dedicated to social progress through philanthropy and entrepreneurship in the arts. She is currently administrative director of the Frederick Hammersley Foundation, coadministrator of *The Lightning Field*, and monthly visual arts contributor to *Arts and Culture Texas*. Her most recent endeavors include Pacific Exhibits, a storefront window micro-gallery, and Show Up Show Down, a quick-response mechanism for staging world-changing art through brief photography exhibitions of artist projects that incorporate the built environment, coinciding visiting artist presentations, and an ever-growing publicly accessible archive. In late 2014, she opened Central Features, a contemporary art venue in downtown Albuquerque. Nancy also sits on the board of Downtown Albuquerque Arts & Cultural District and is the regional coordinator for The Feminist Art Project.

Le LeFever is the founder and creative director of Common Craft and the author of *The Art of Explanation*. He is the son of a goldfish farmer and the husband of Sachi LeFever, who is his partner in crime at Common Craft. They live and work in Seattle.

Jeff Wysaki is a humor writer, comic artist, and blogger based in Los Angeles. He runs the popular website Pleated-Jeans.com. Stuff he makes is routinely featured on the front page of Reddit, The Huffington Post, BuzzFeed, and more, MORE (much MORE!).

Zach Weinersmith is best known for his comic strip *Saturday Morning Breakfast Cereal* and for creating the Festival of Bad Ad hoc Hypotheses. He lives in Texas with his wife Kelly and daughter Ada.

Acknowledgments

To all of the wonderful people featured in this book and to all of the wonderful people who led us to them, THANK YOU OODLES.

Hugs & high-fives,
Jason & Jessica